Scottish Swear Word Coloring Book

By: Shazza T. Jones

I0481359

Introduction

Learn some Scottish swear words while you sit back and colour the pages.

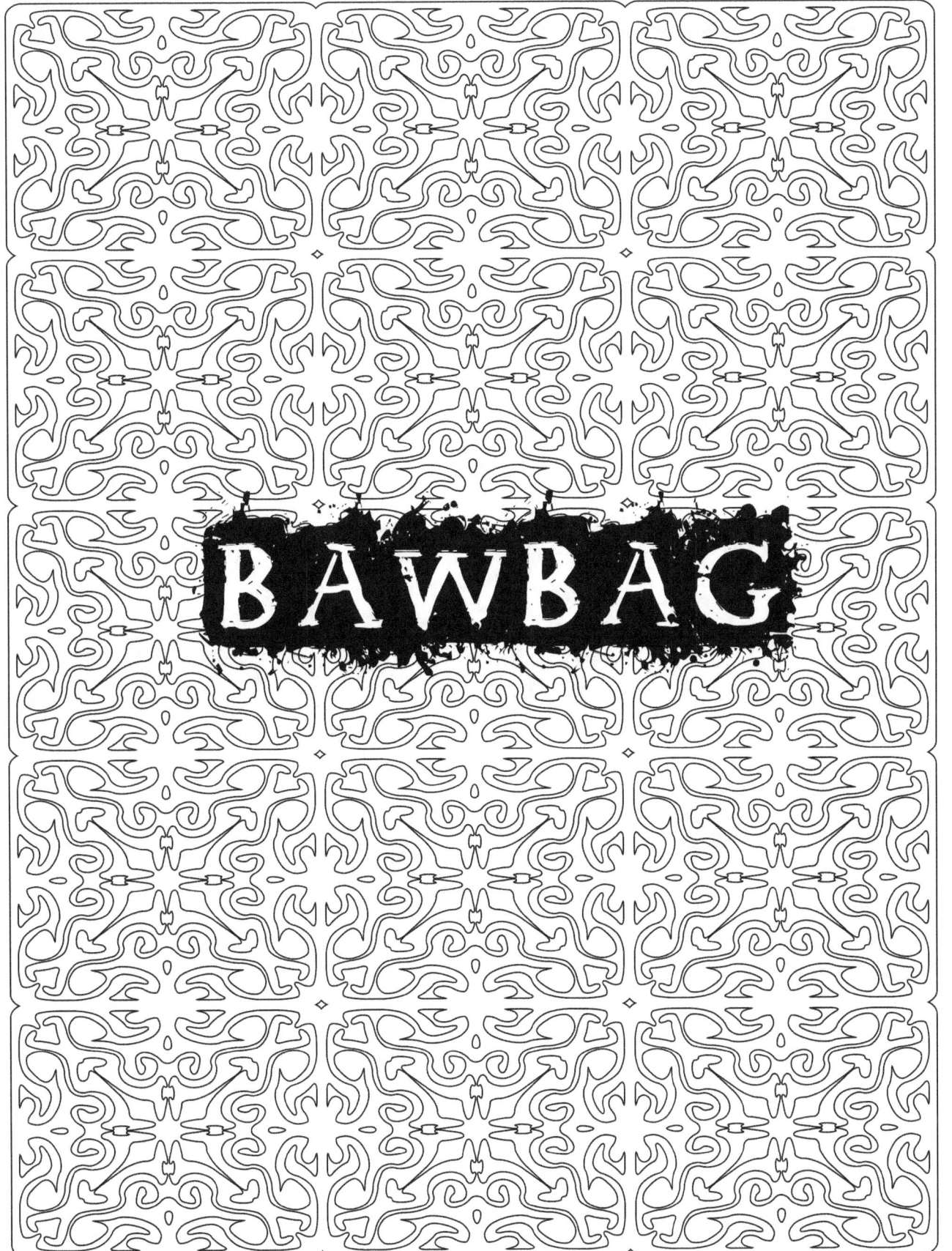

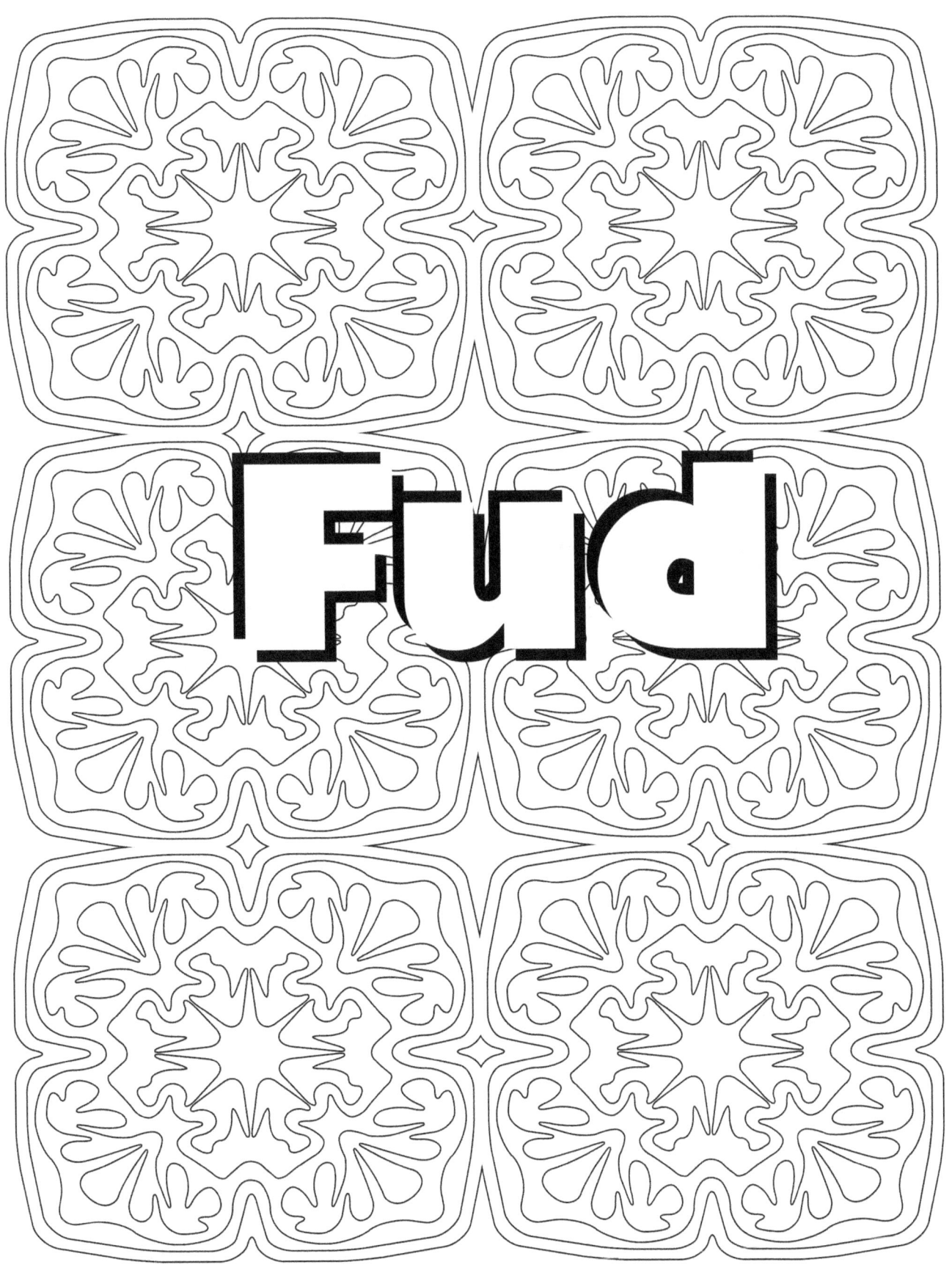

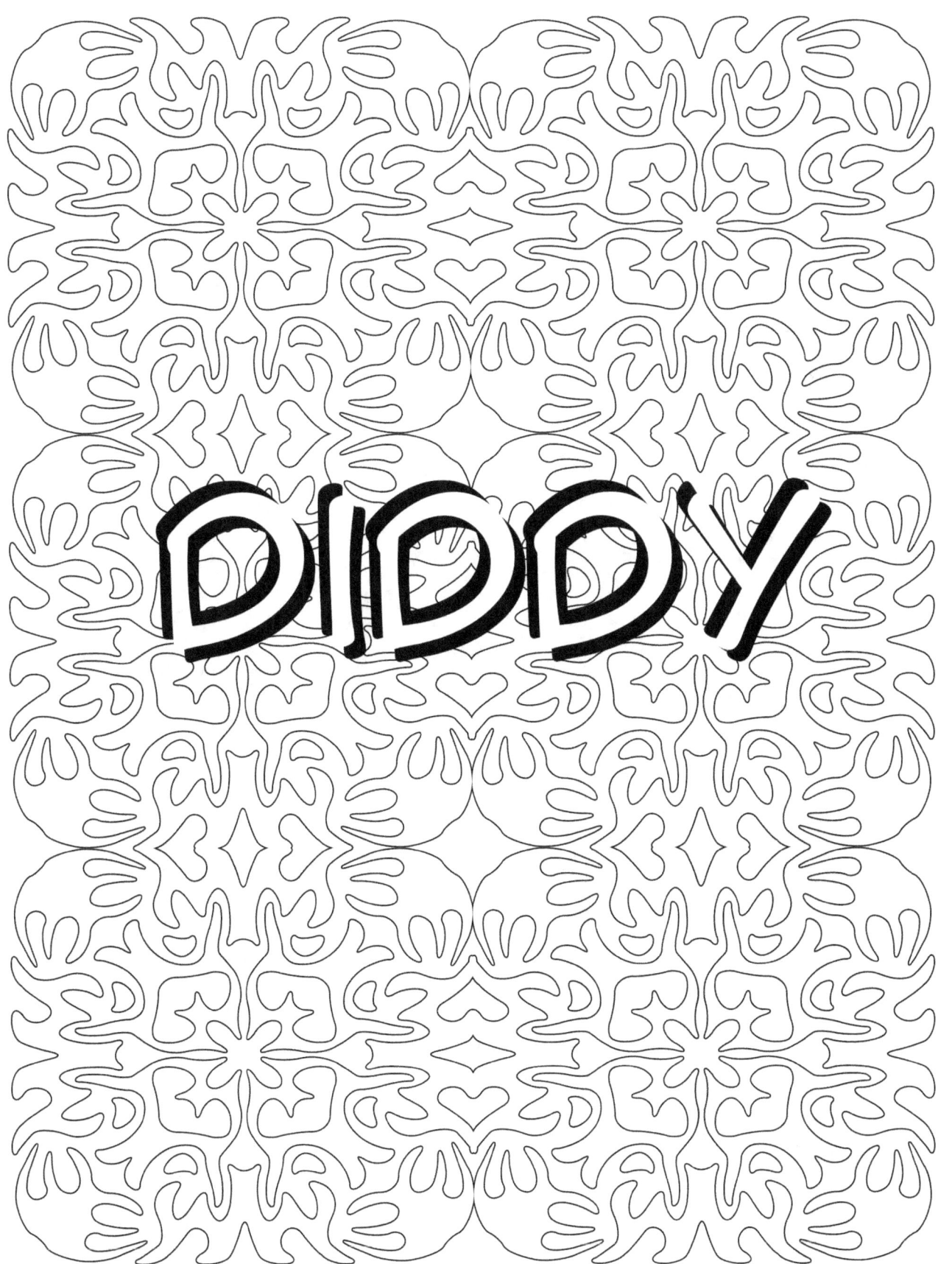

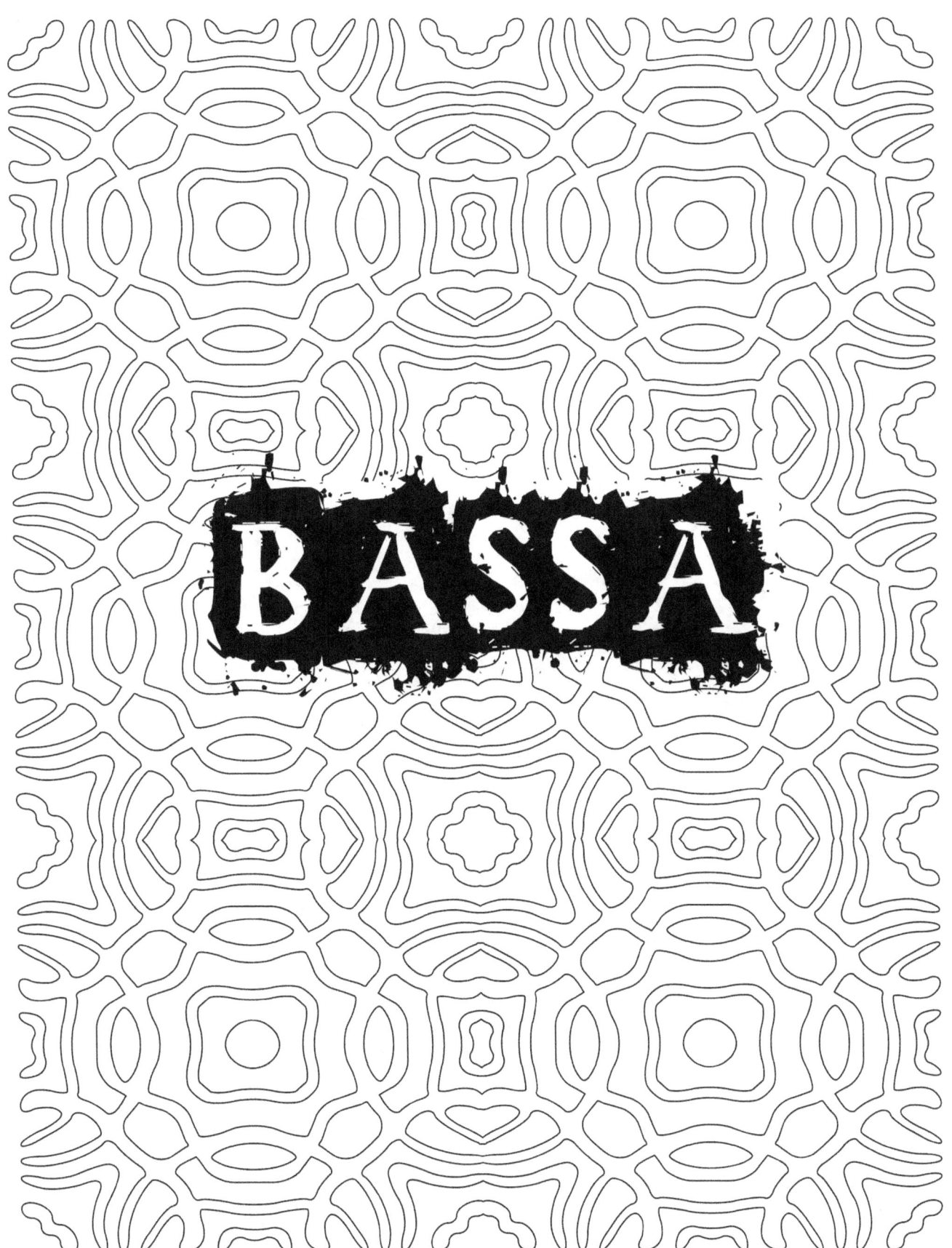

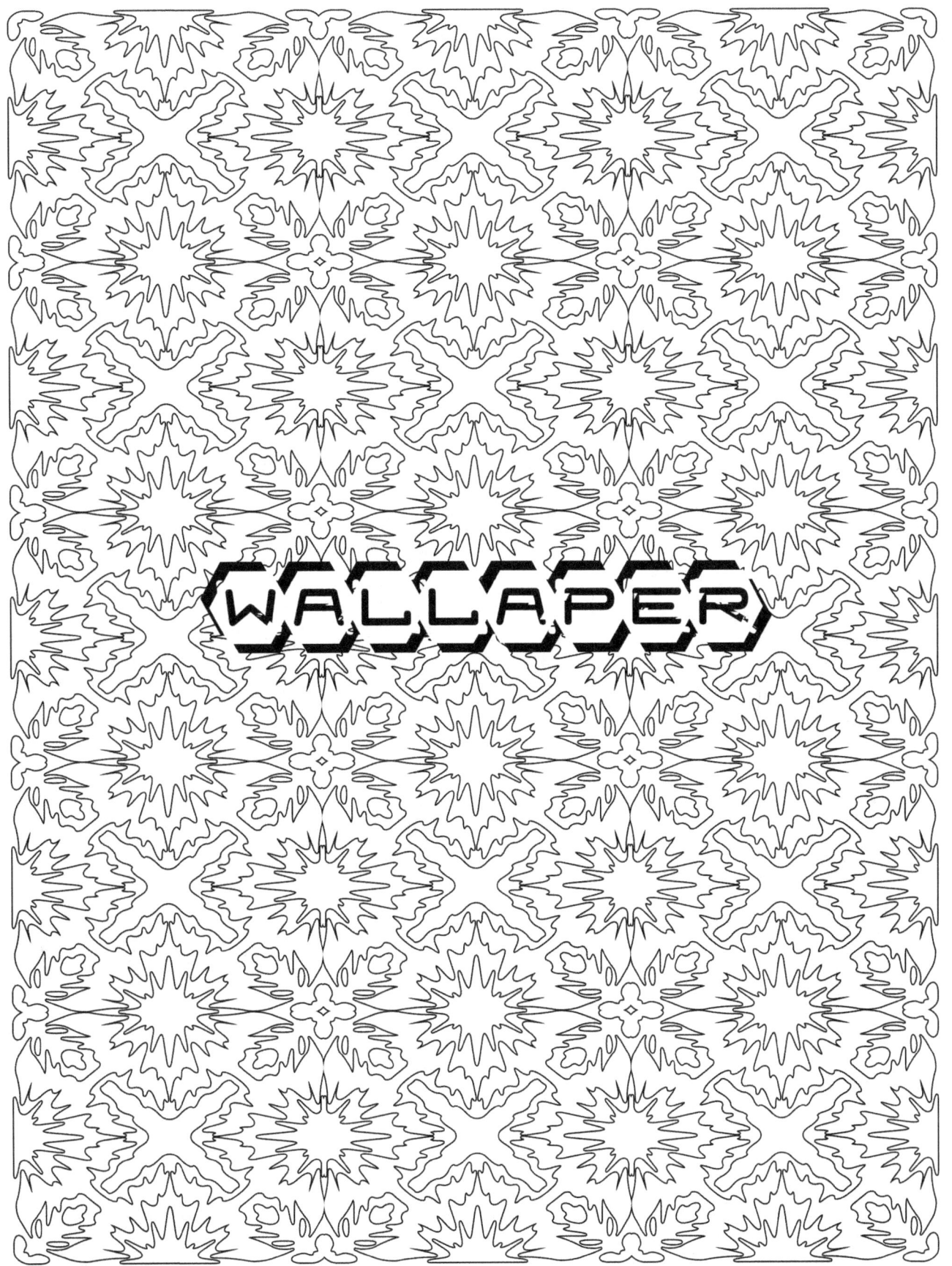

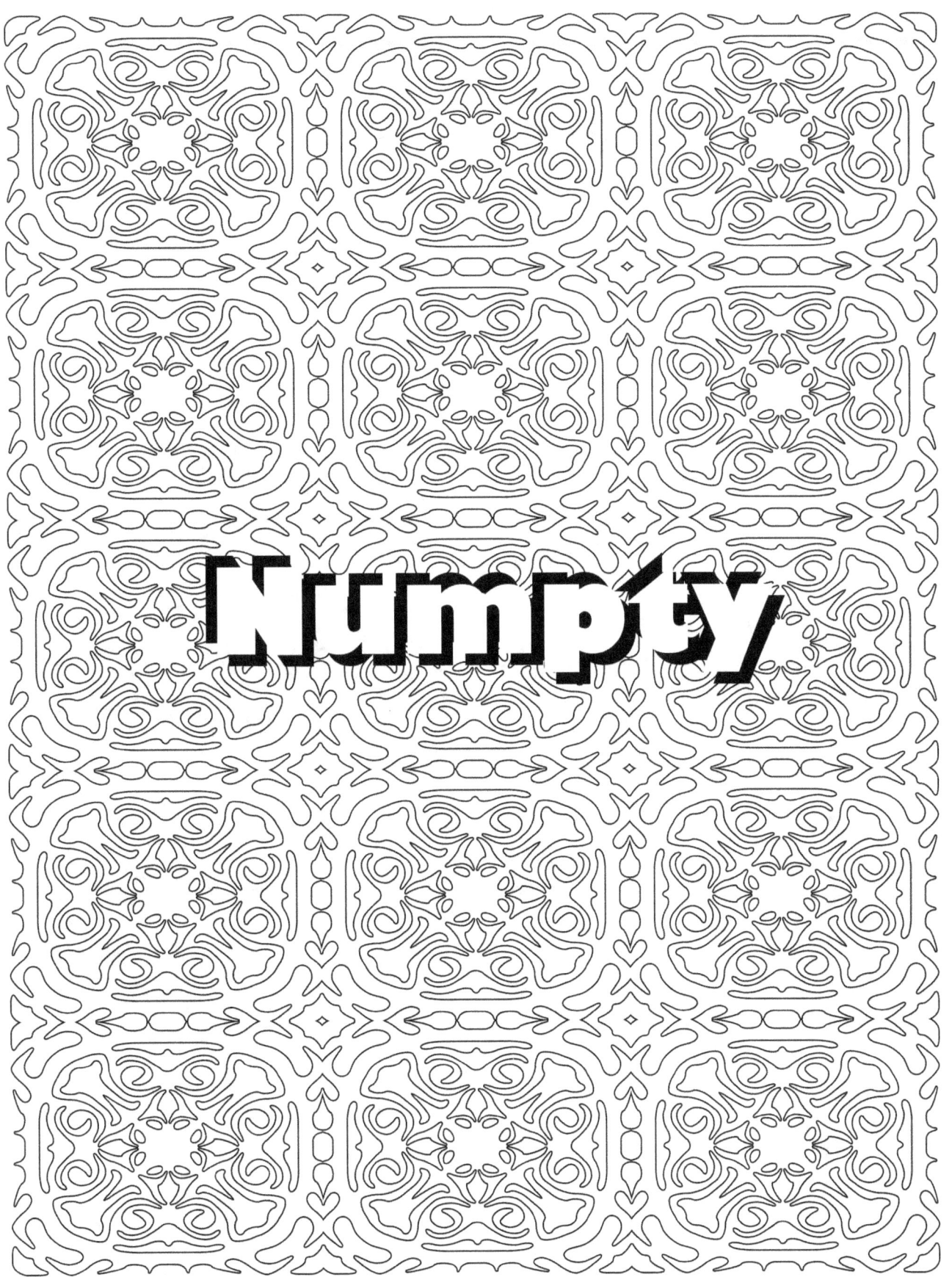

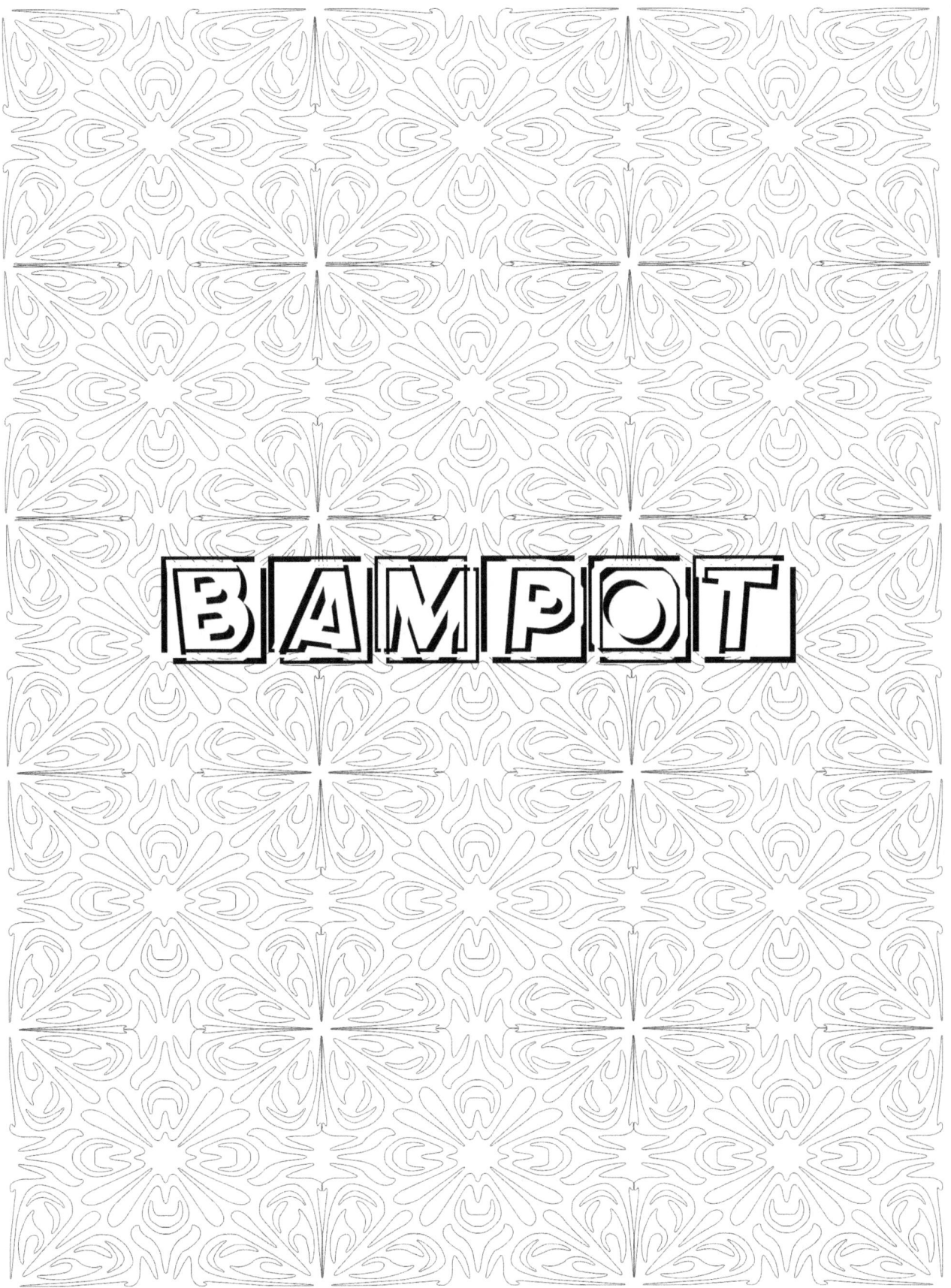

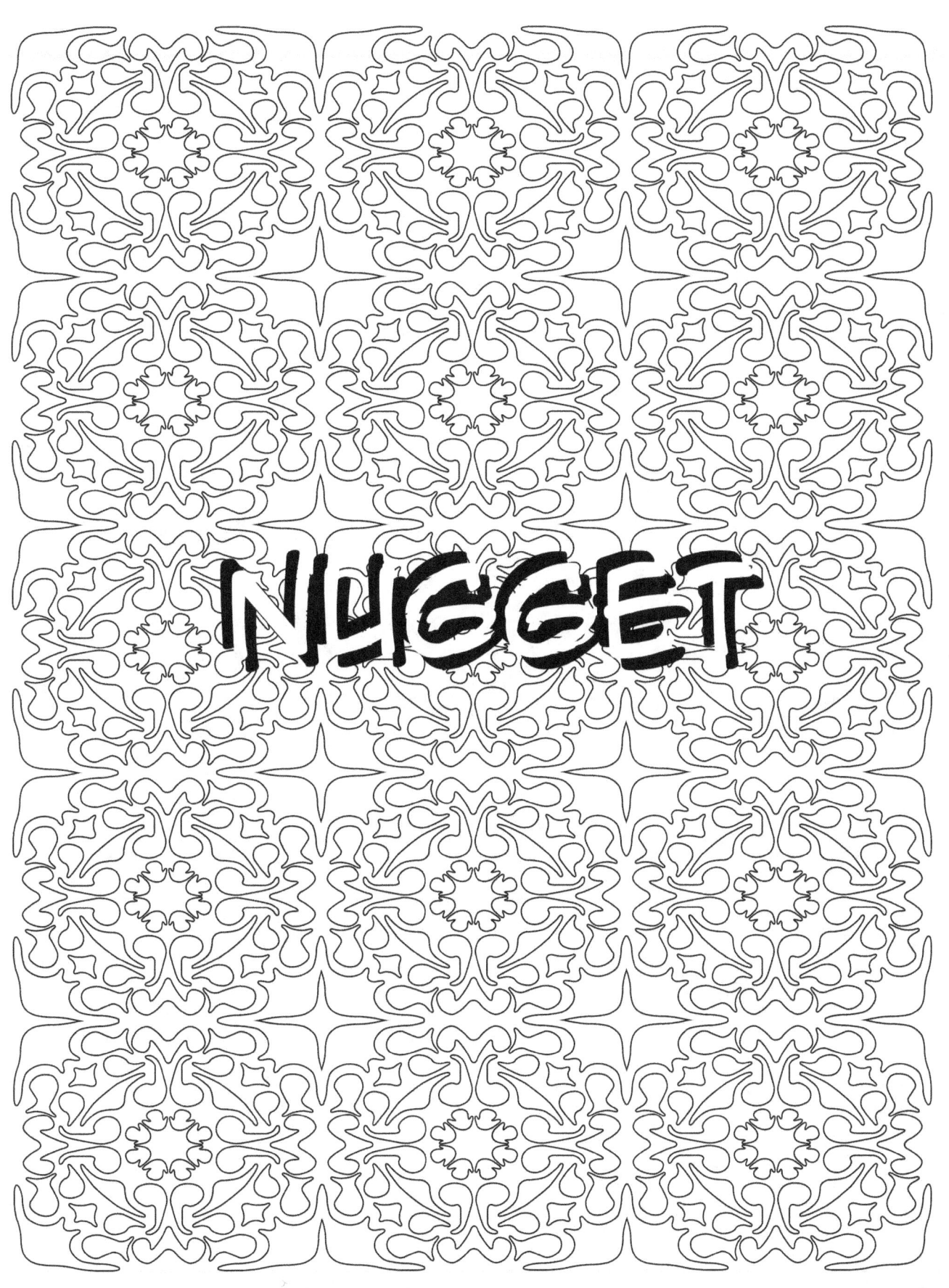

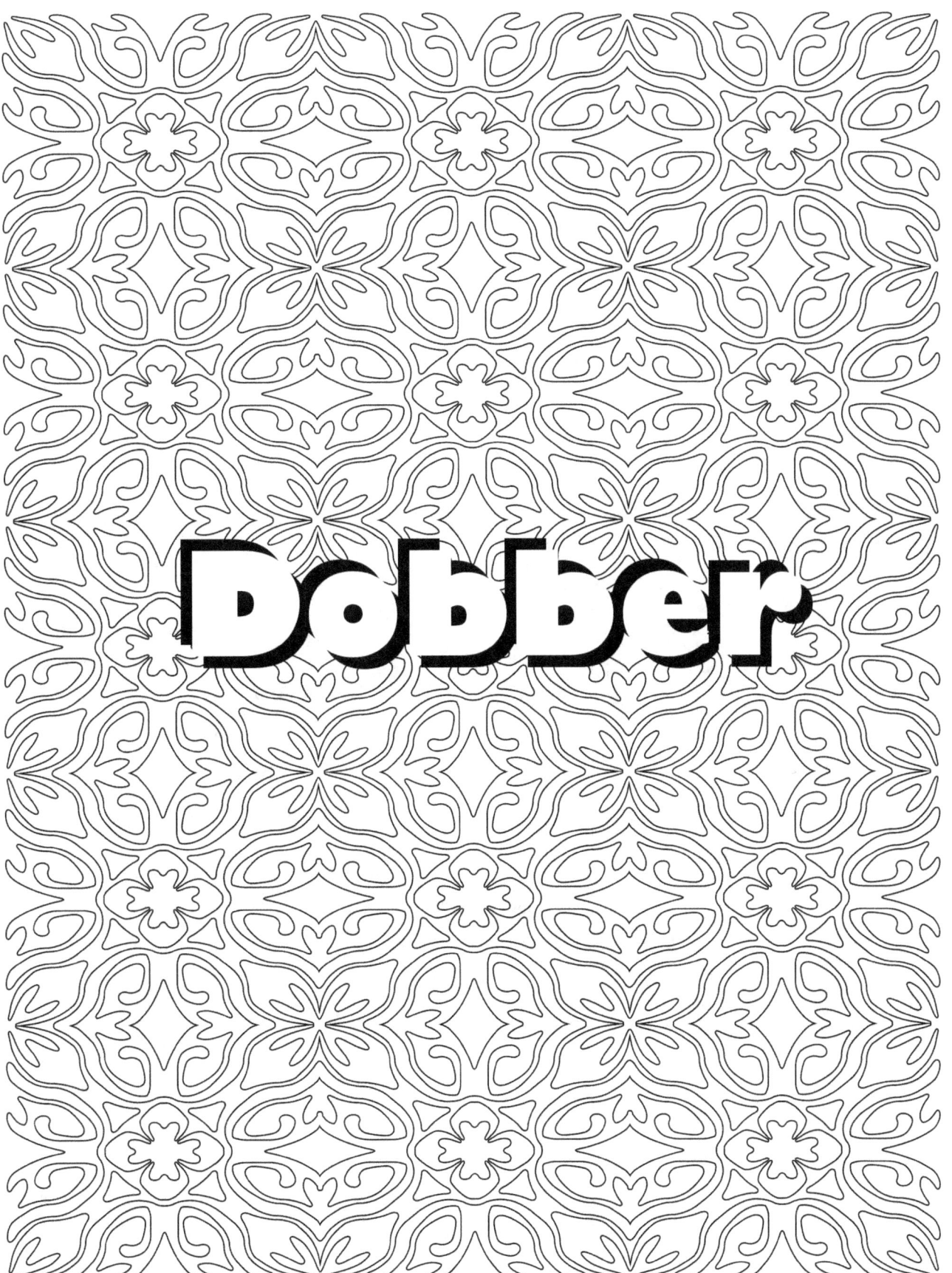

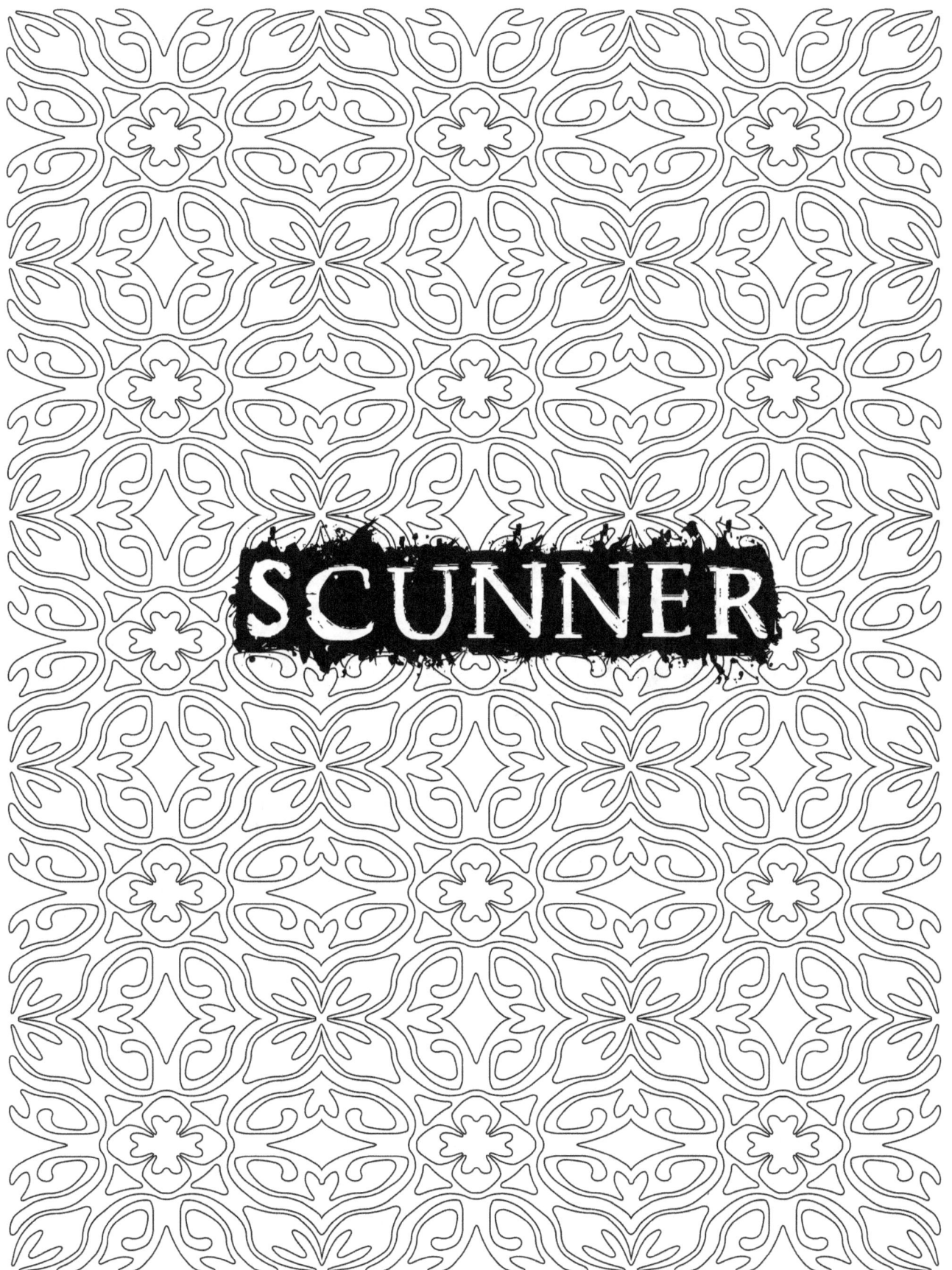

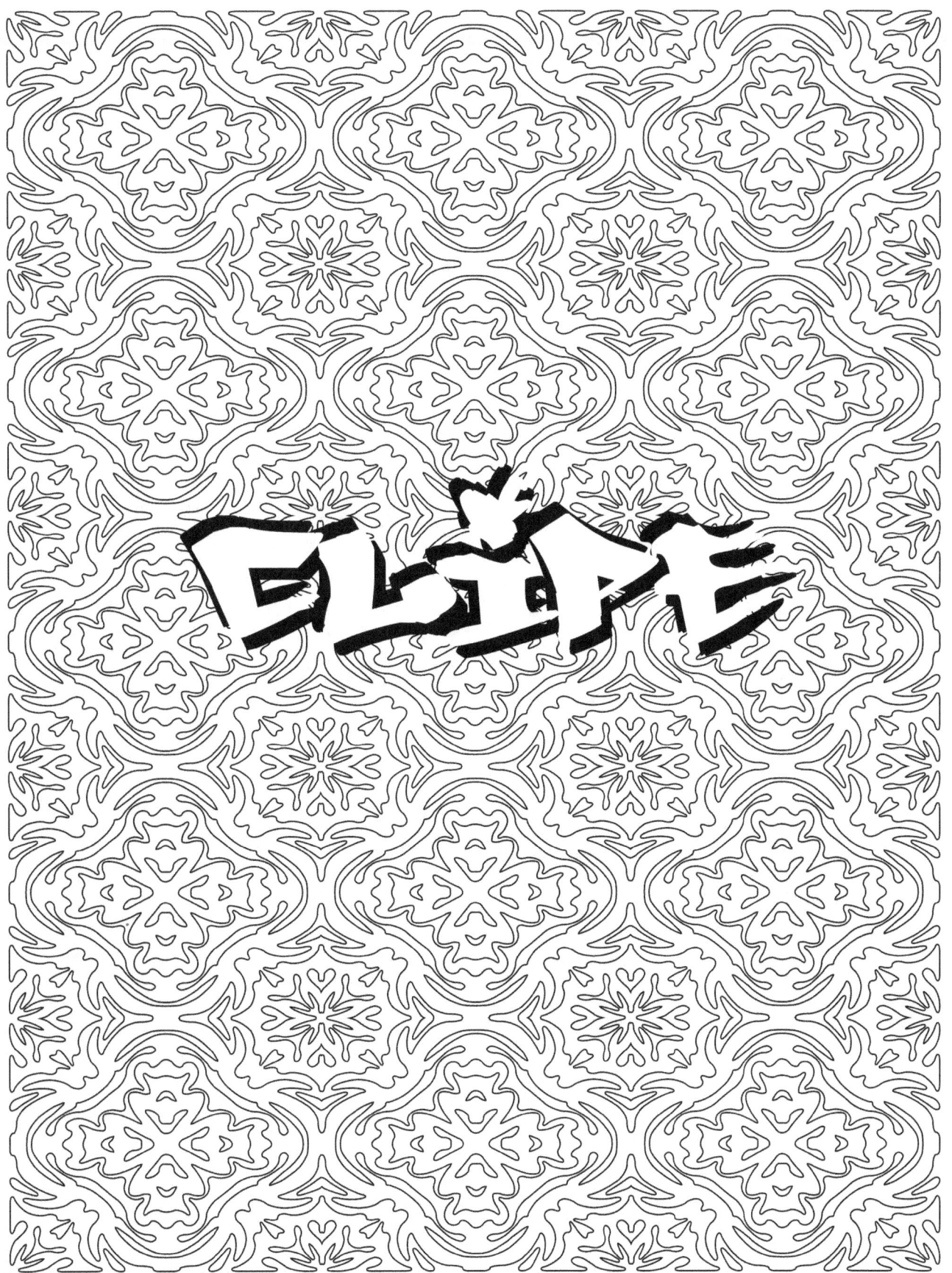

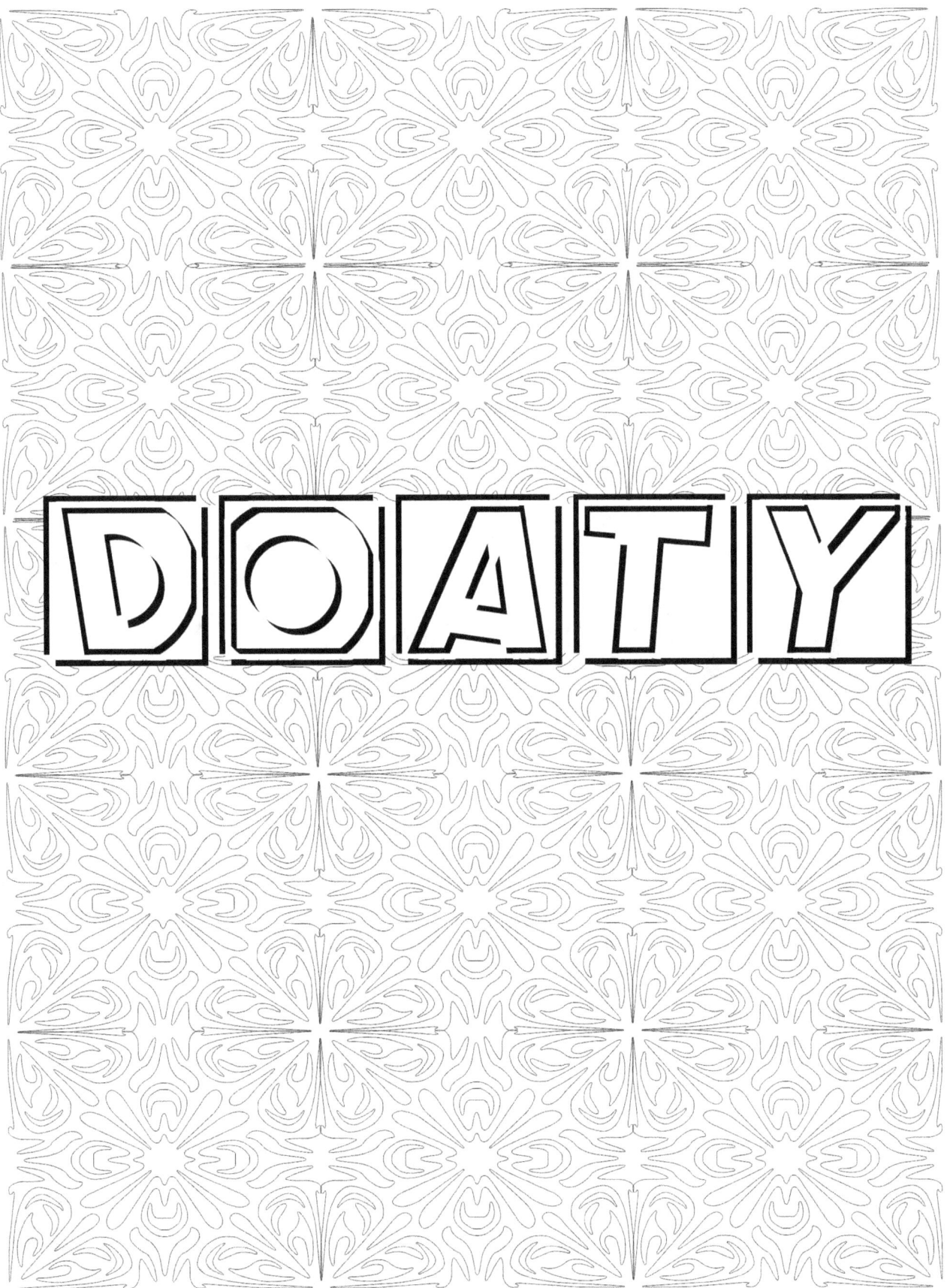

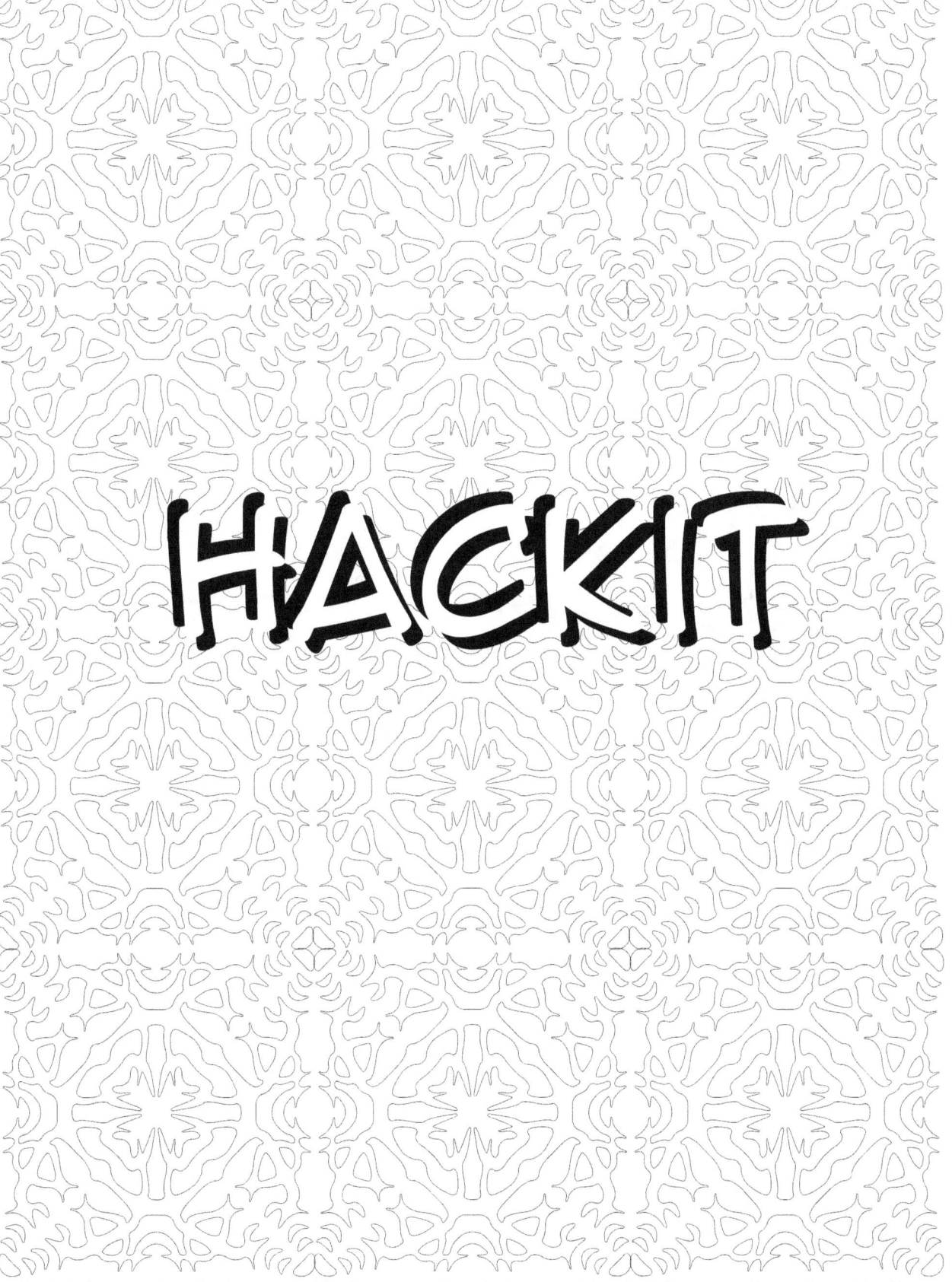

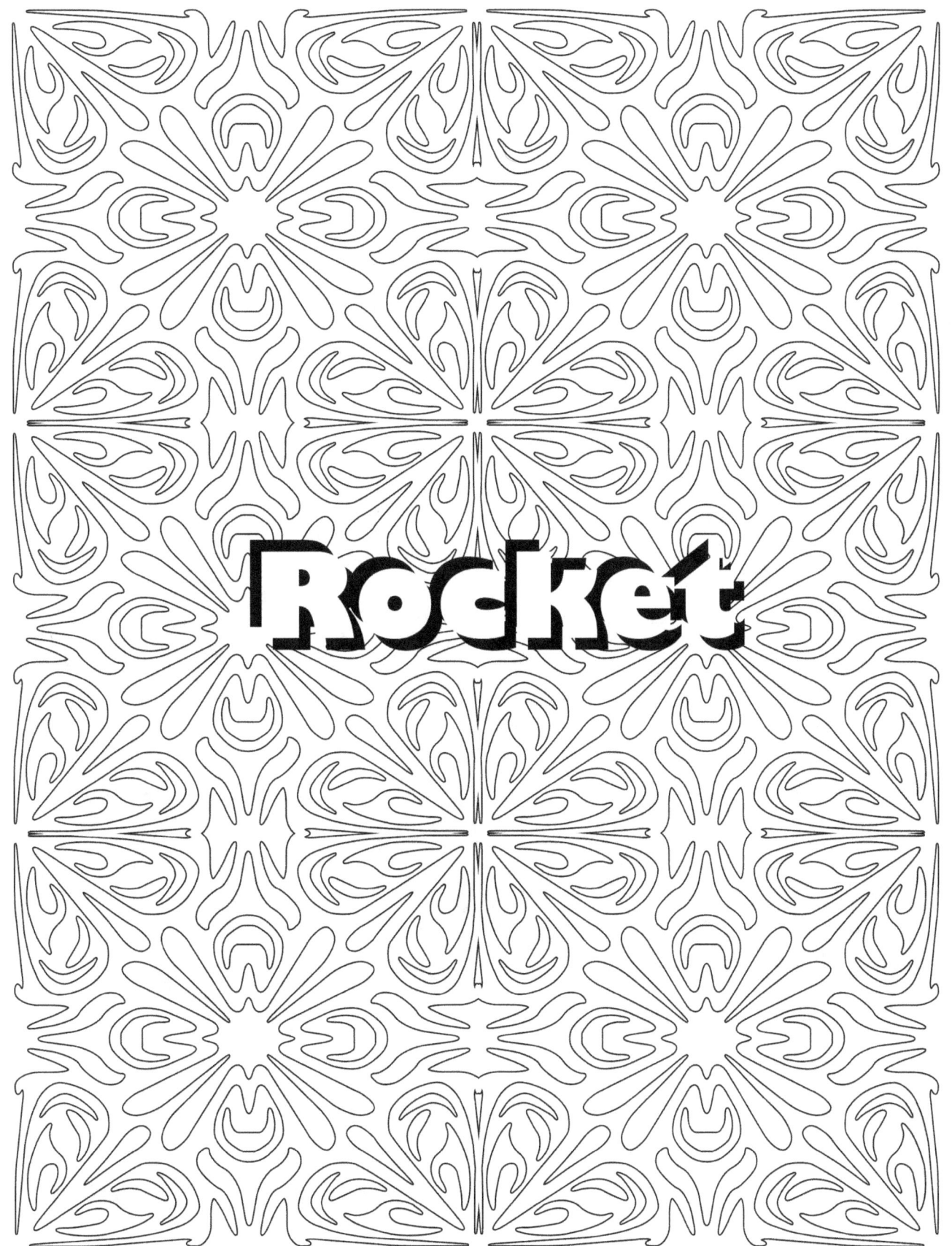

Rocket

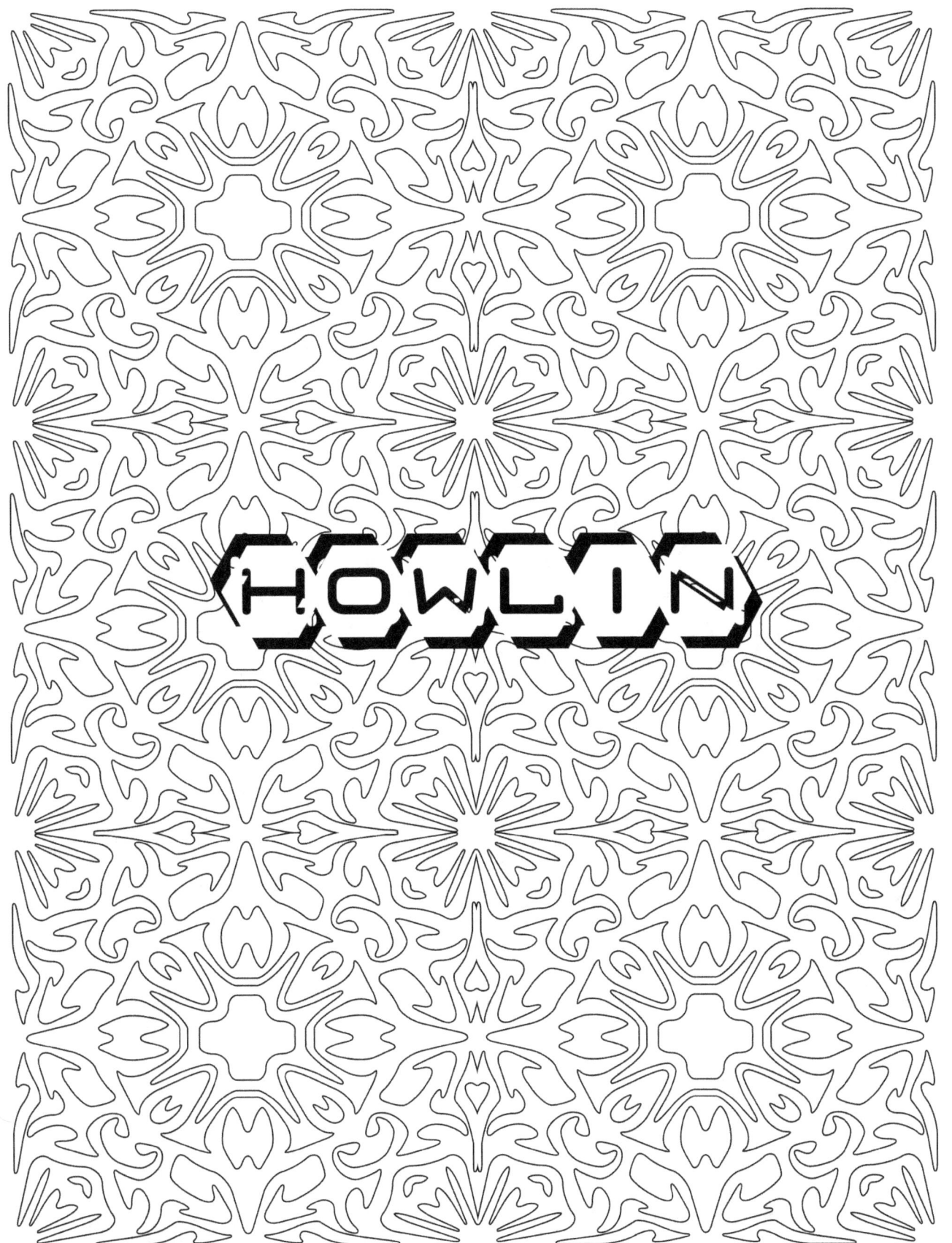

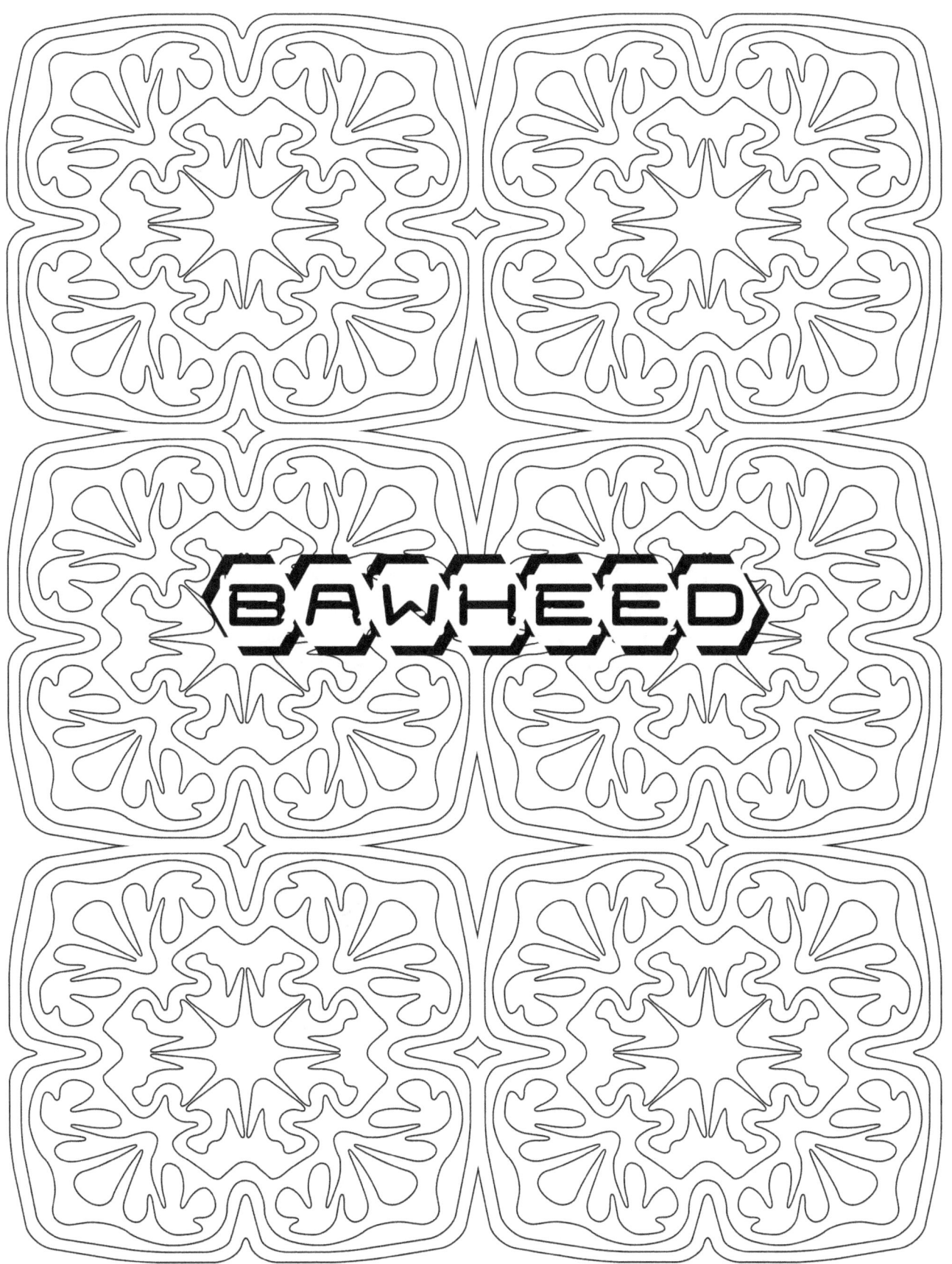

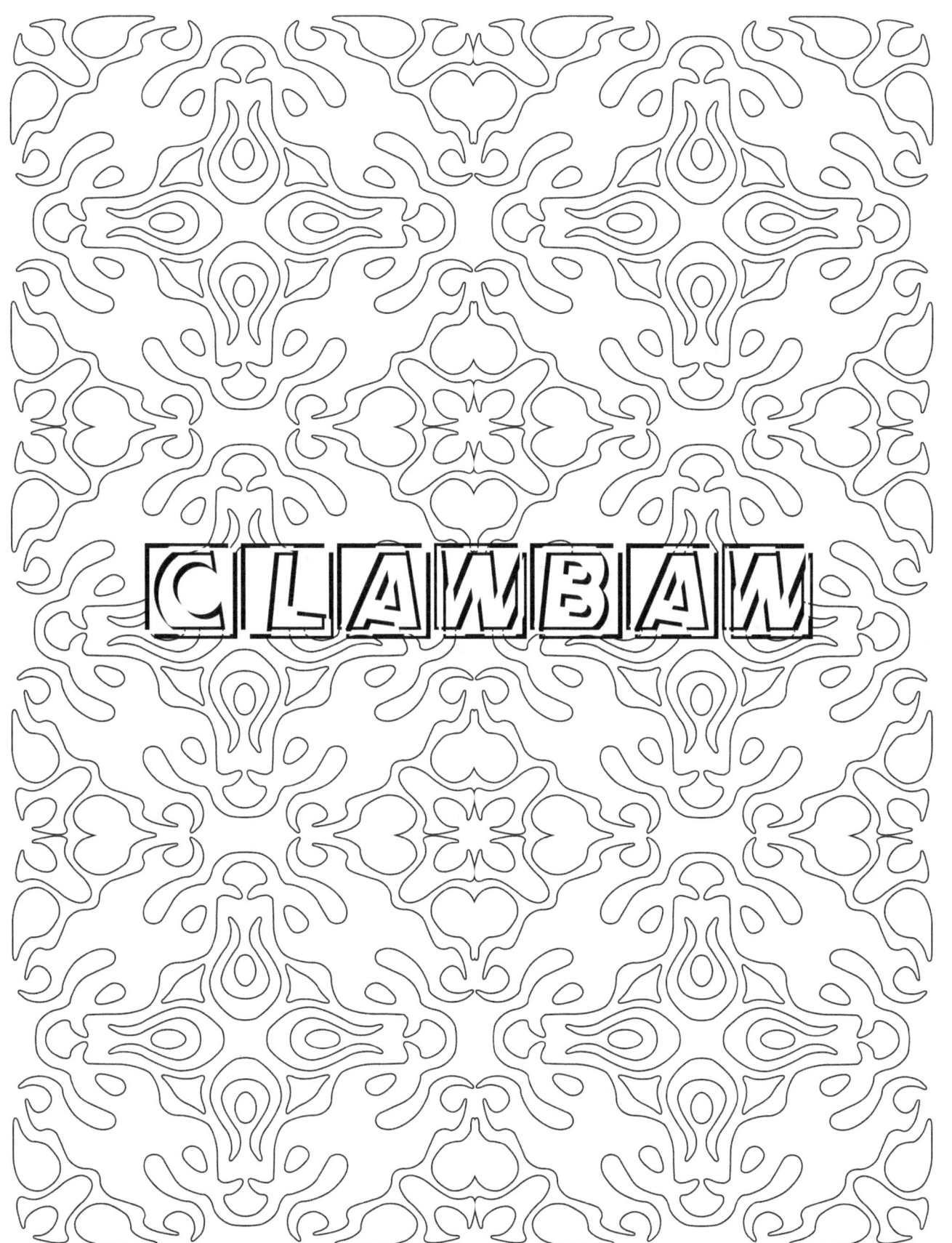

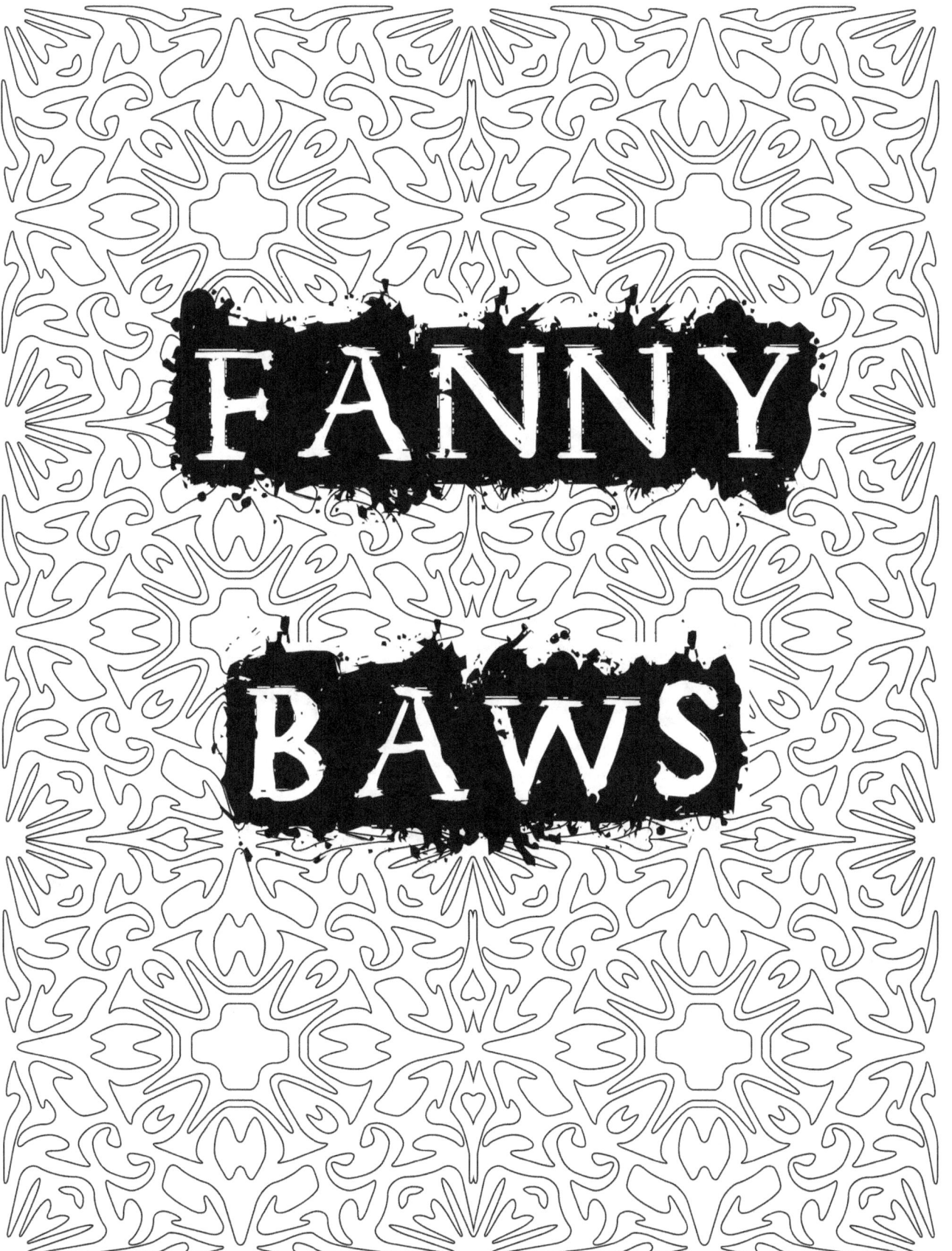

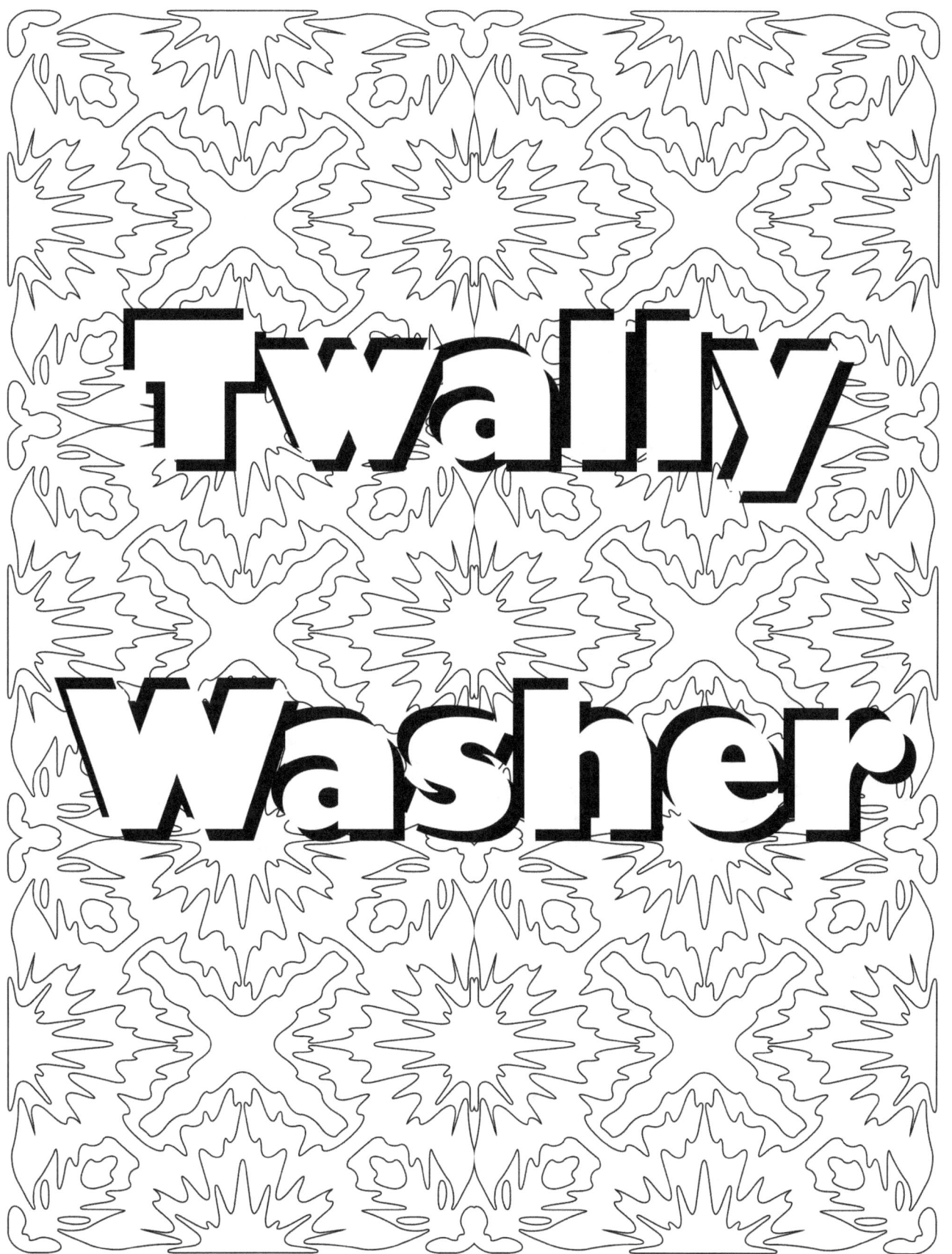

Twally
Washer

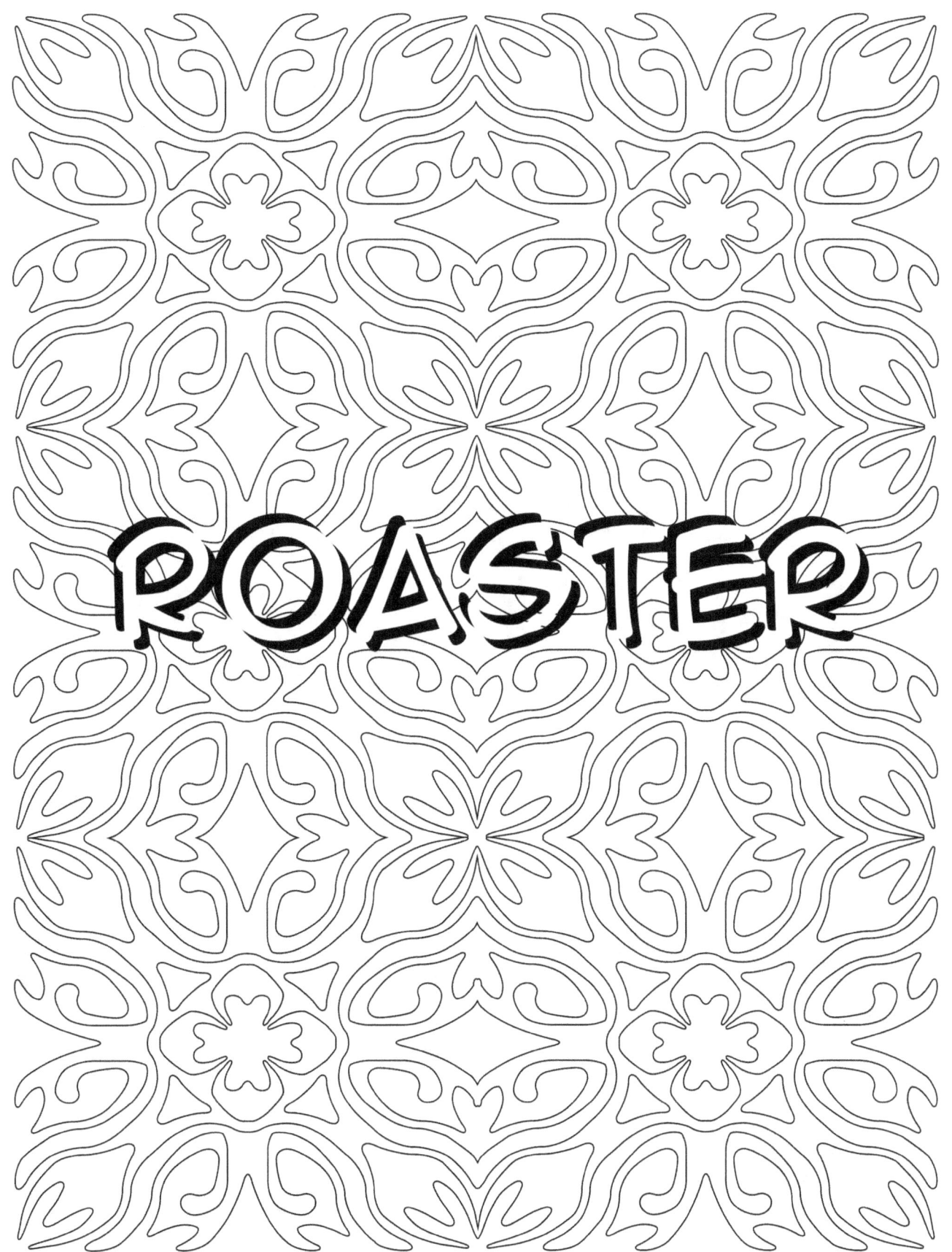

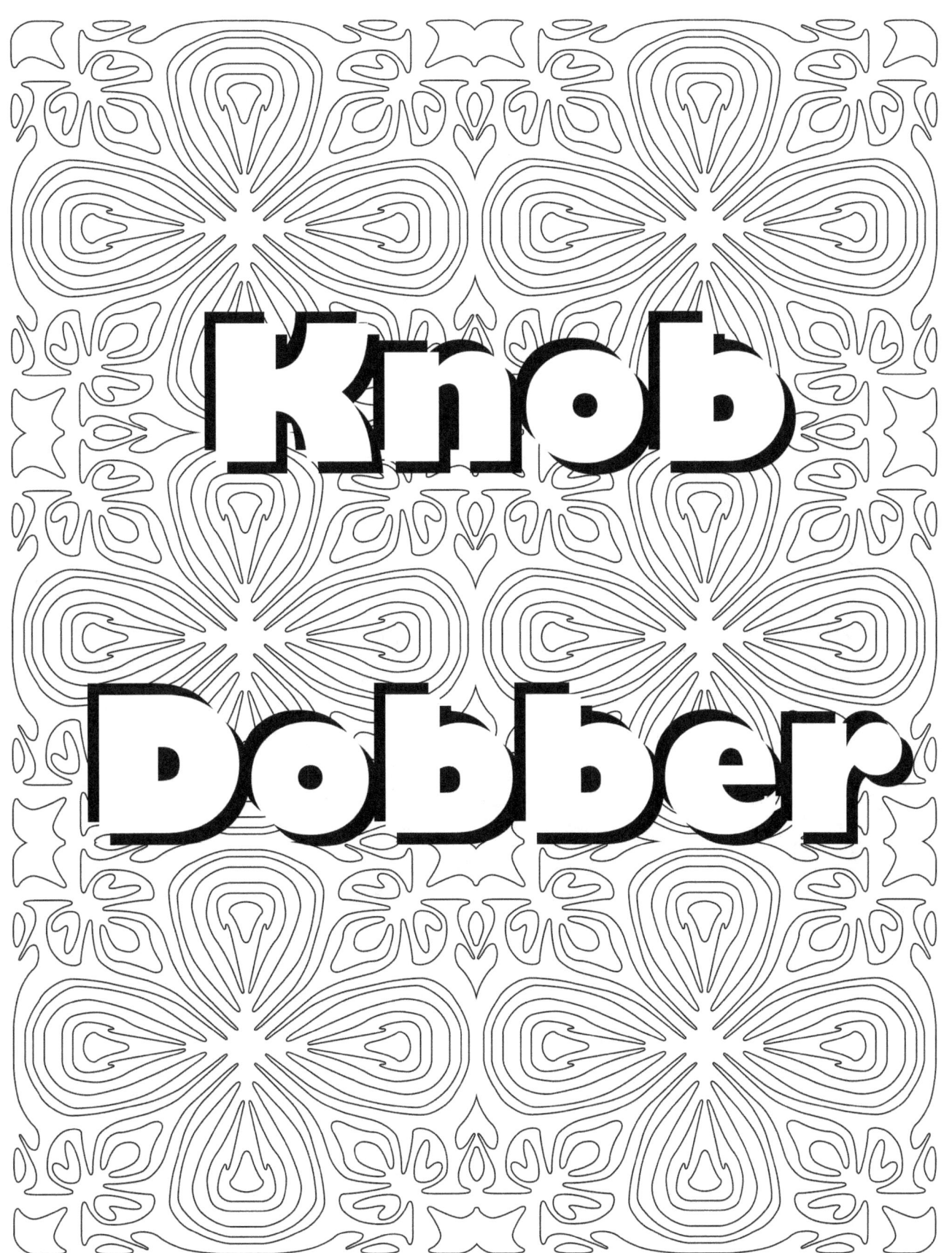

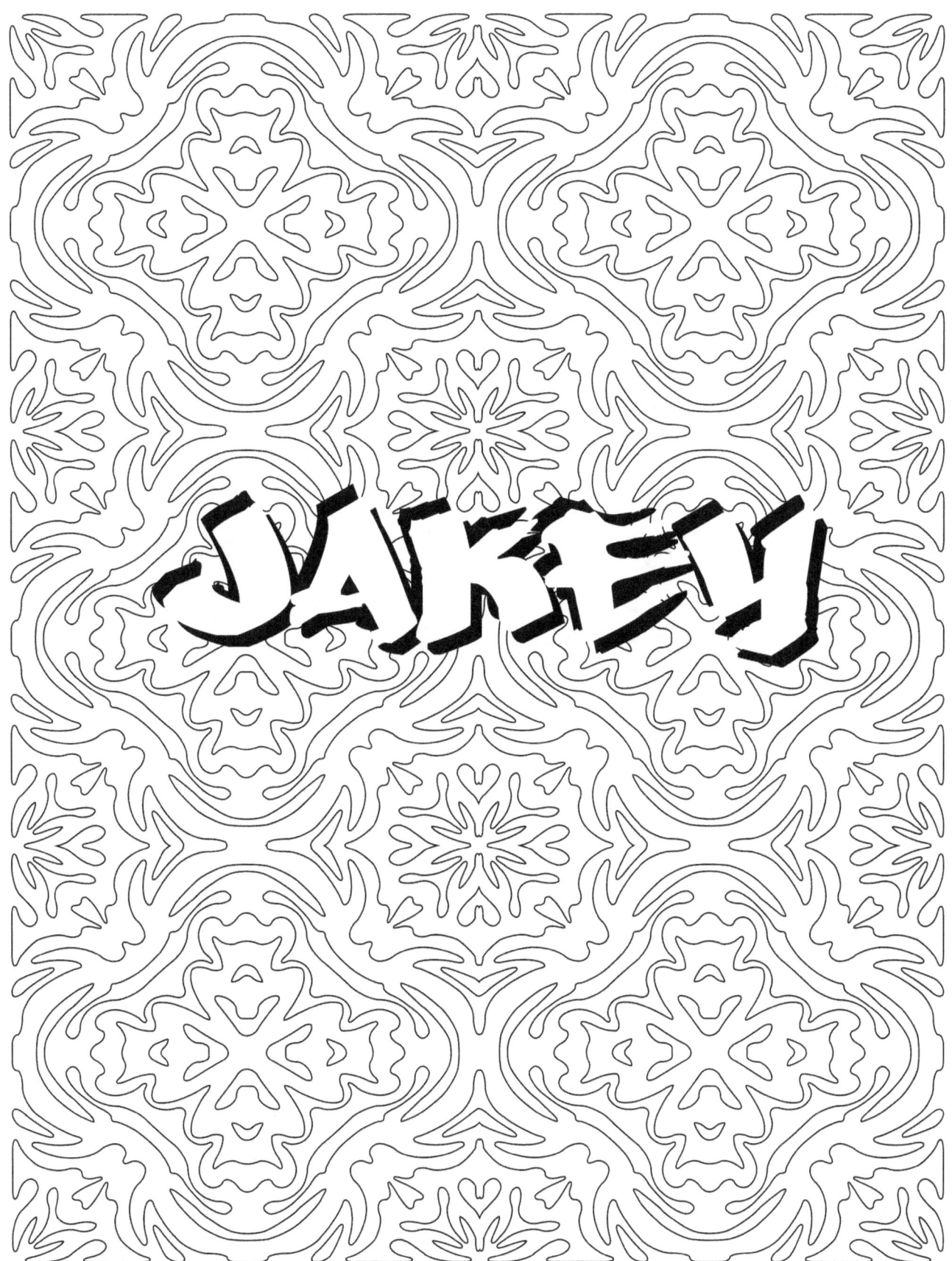

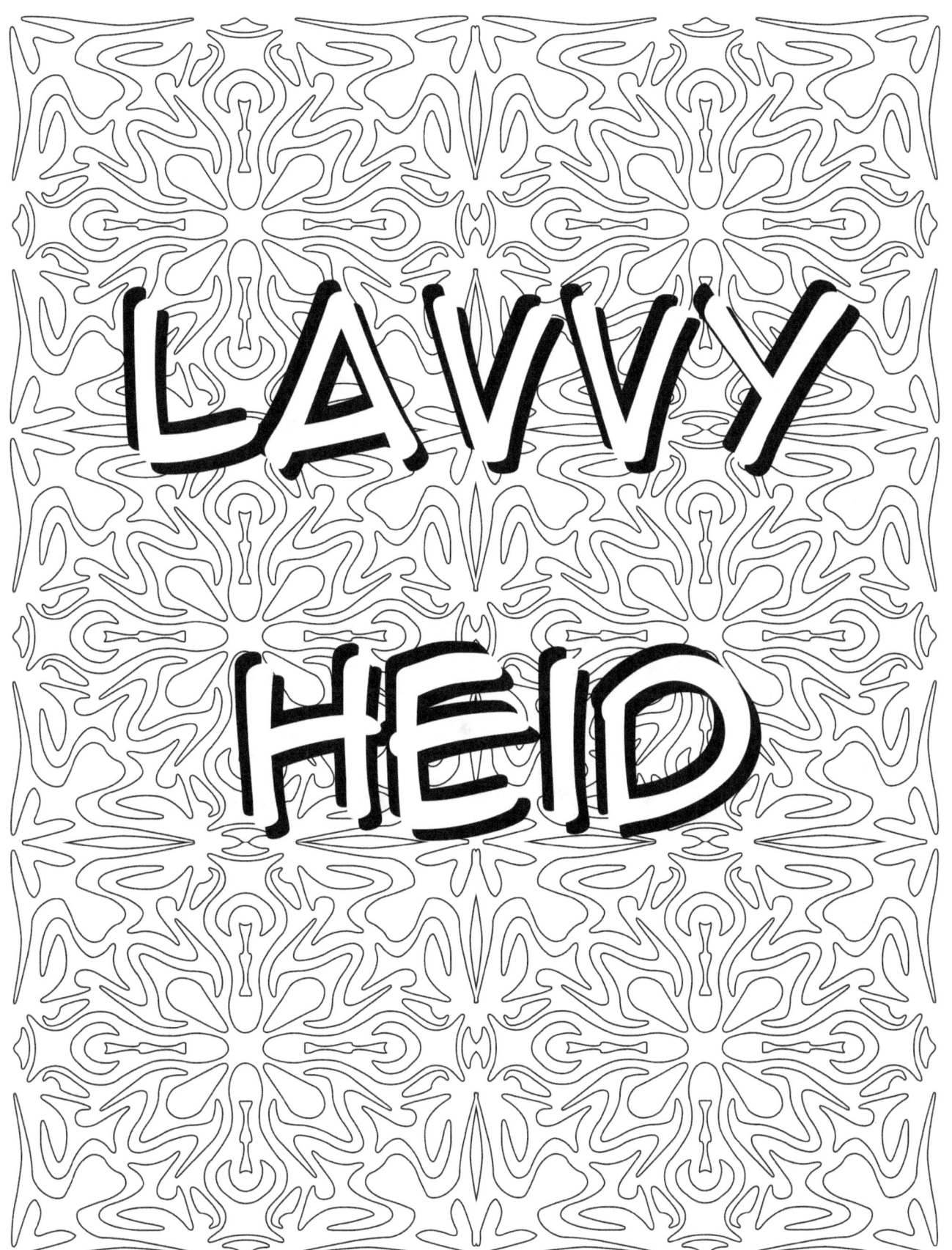

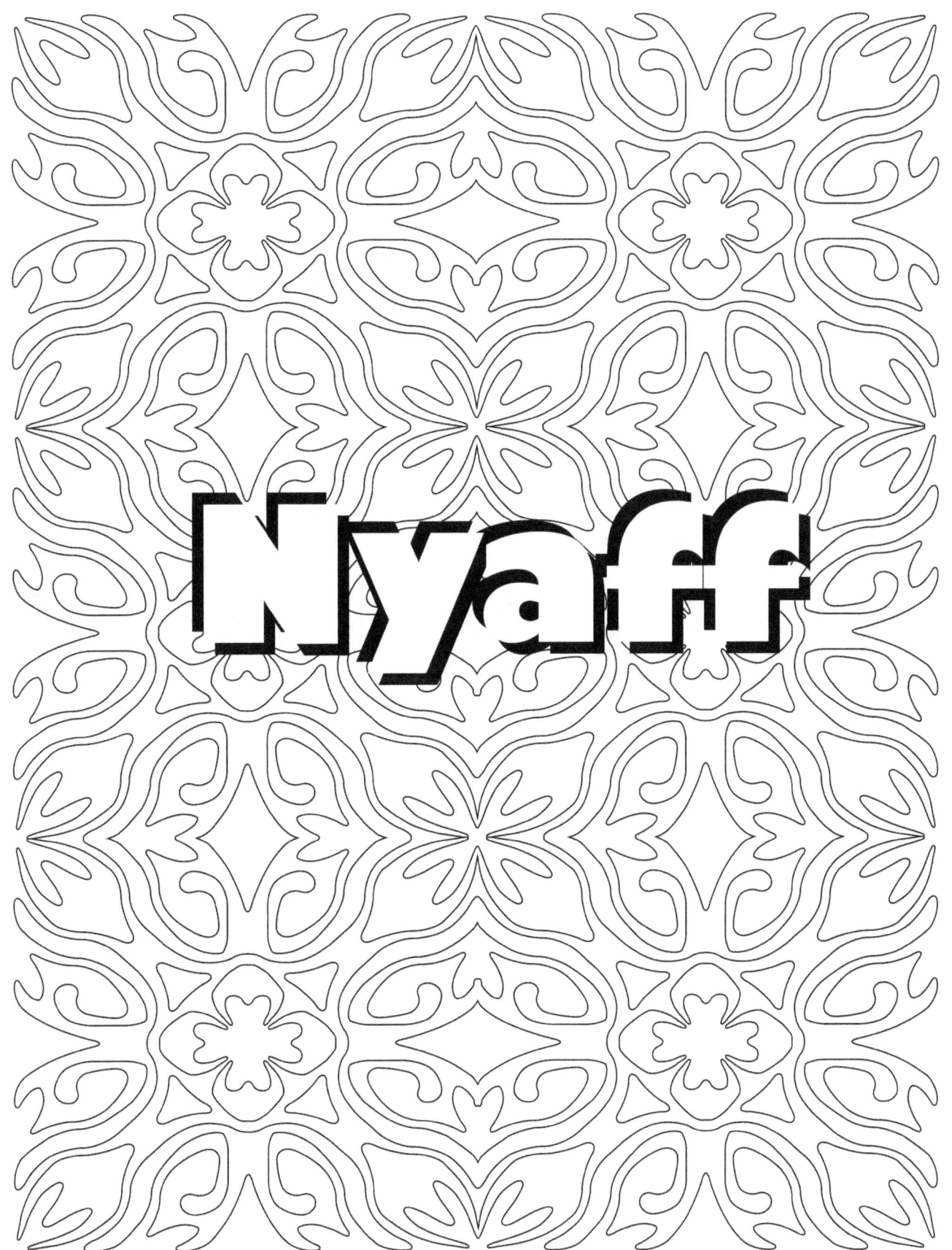

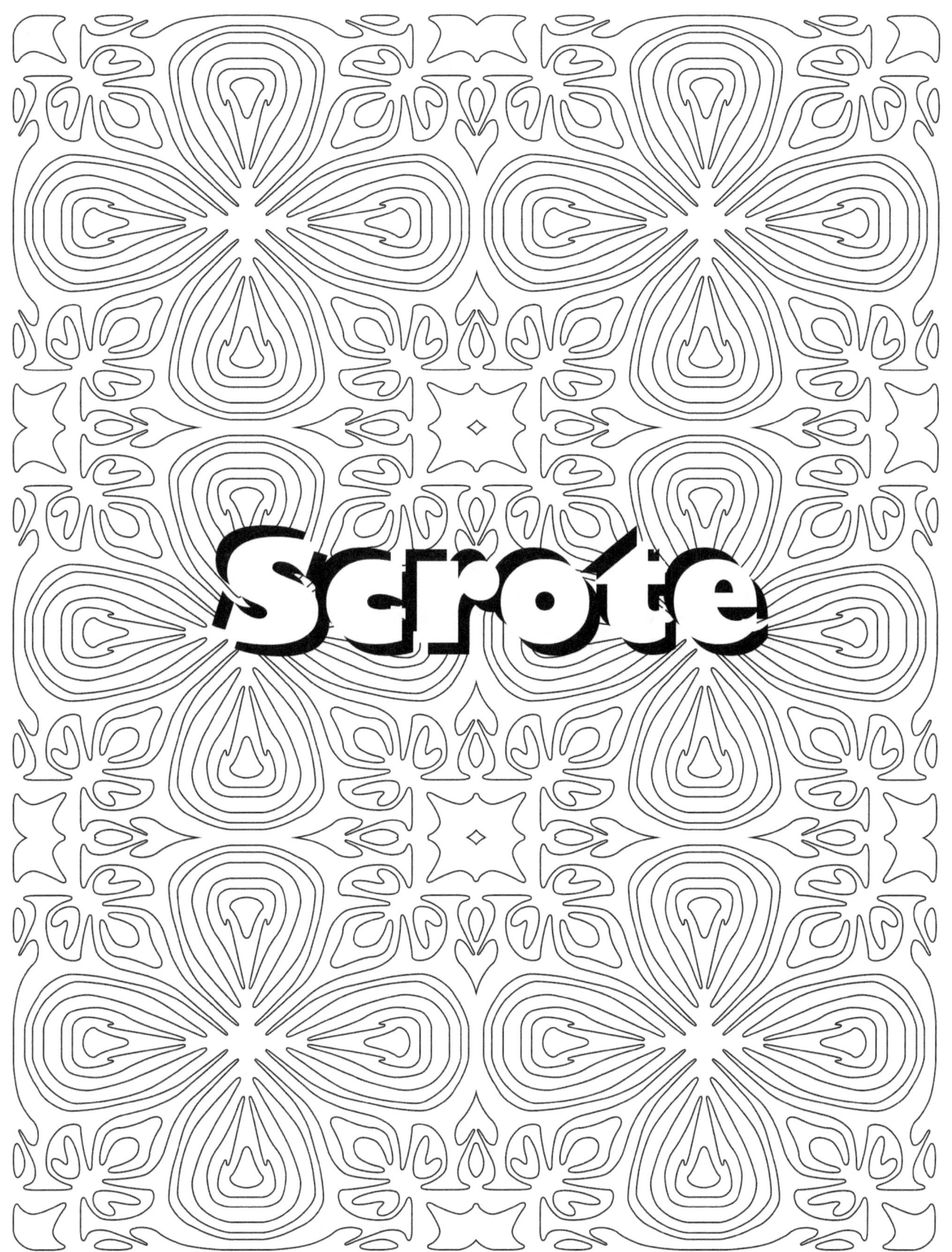

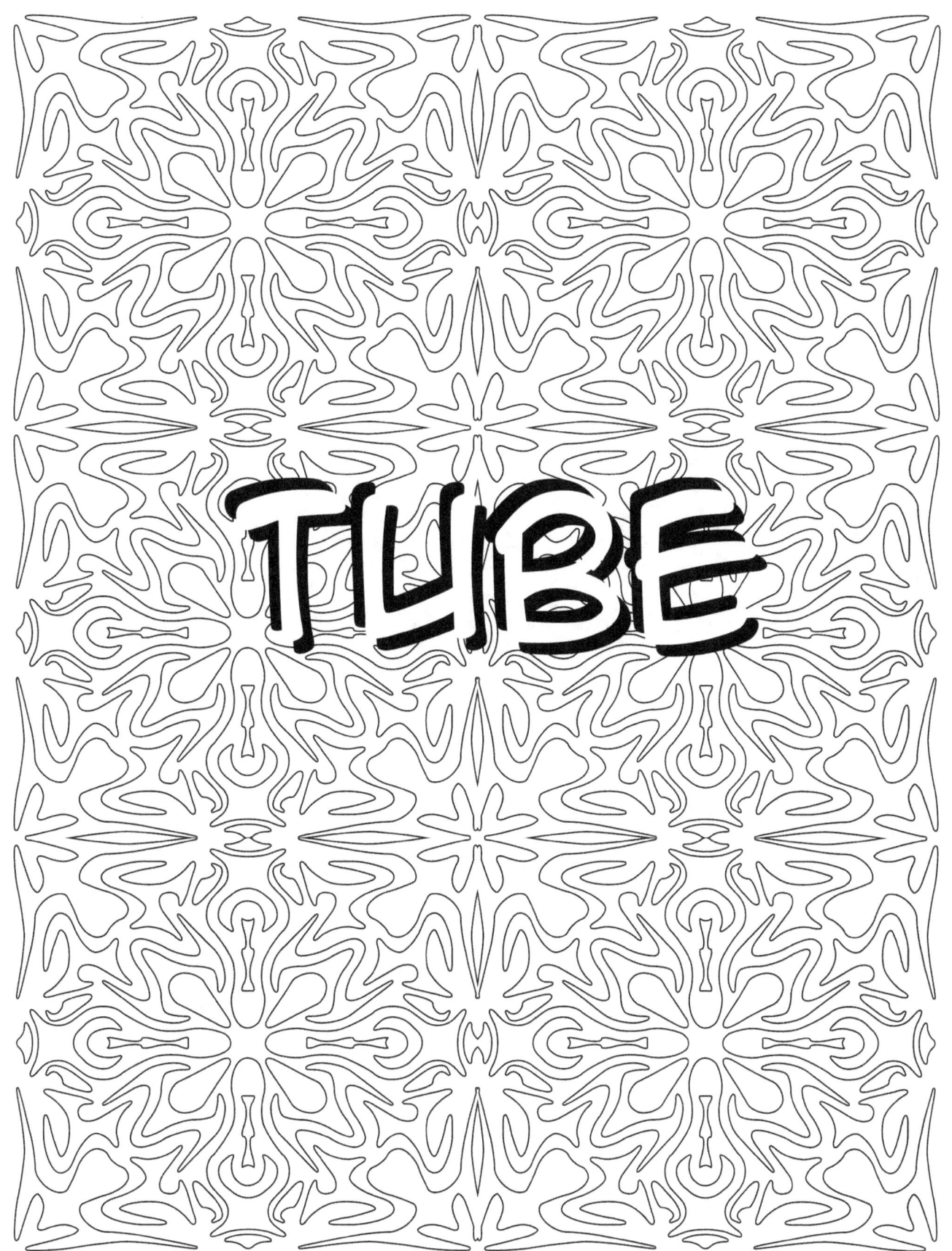

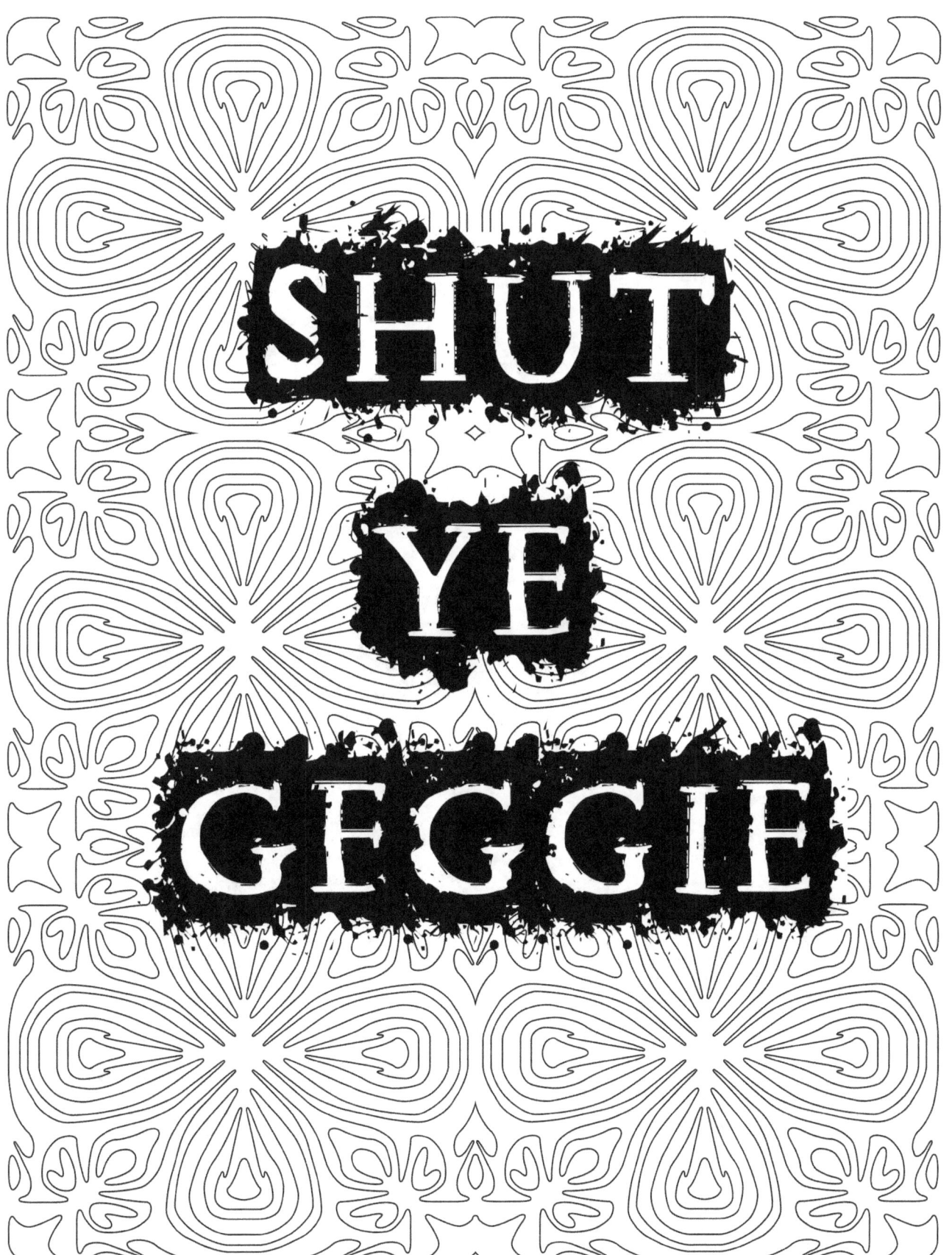

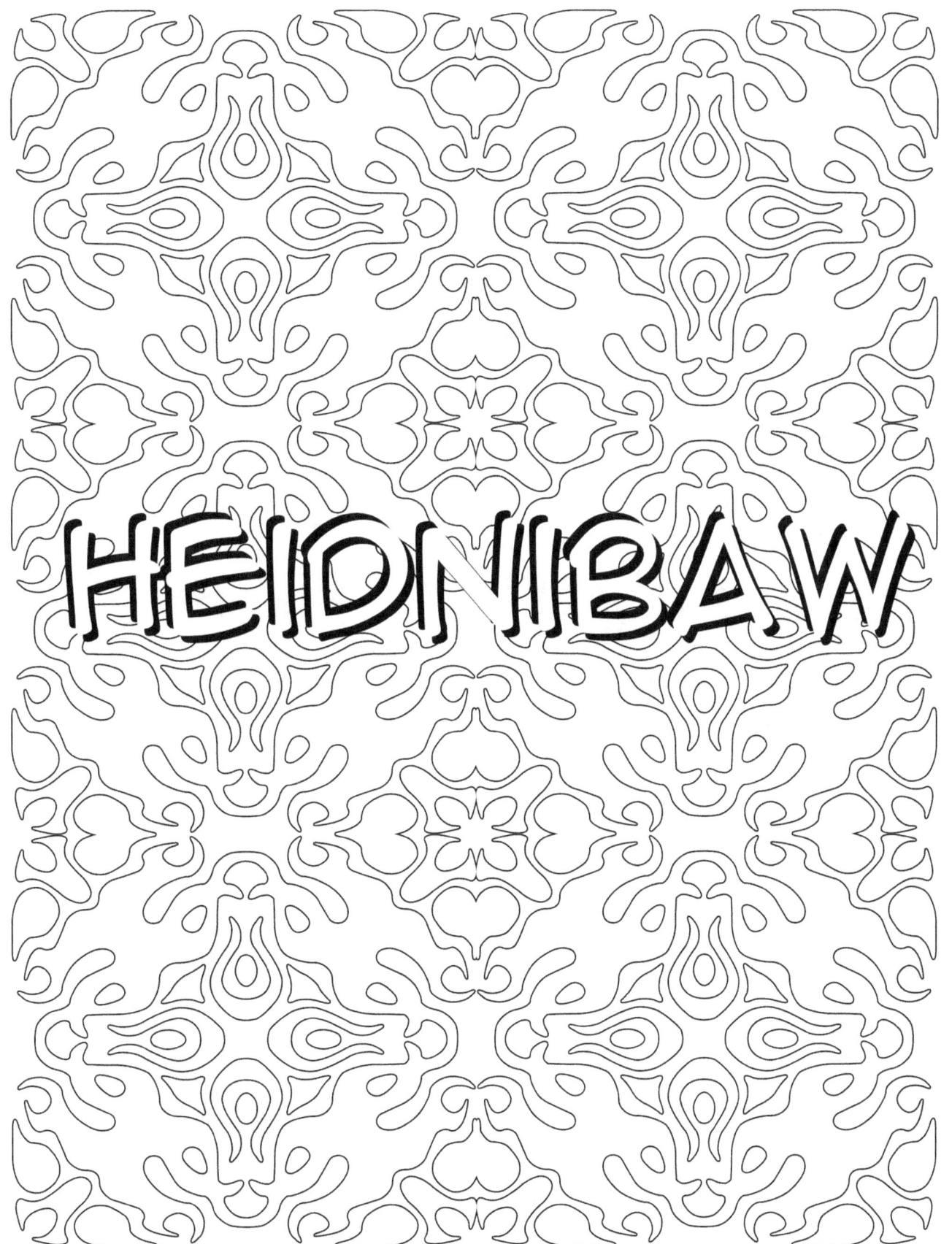

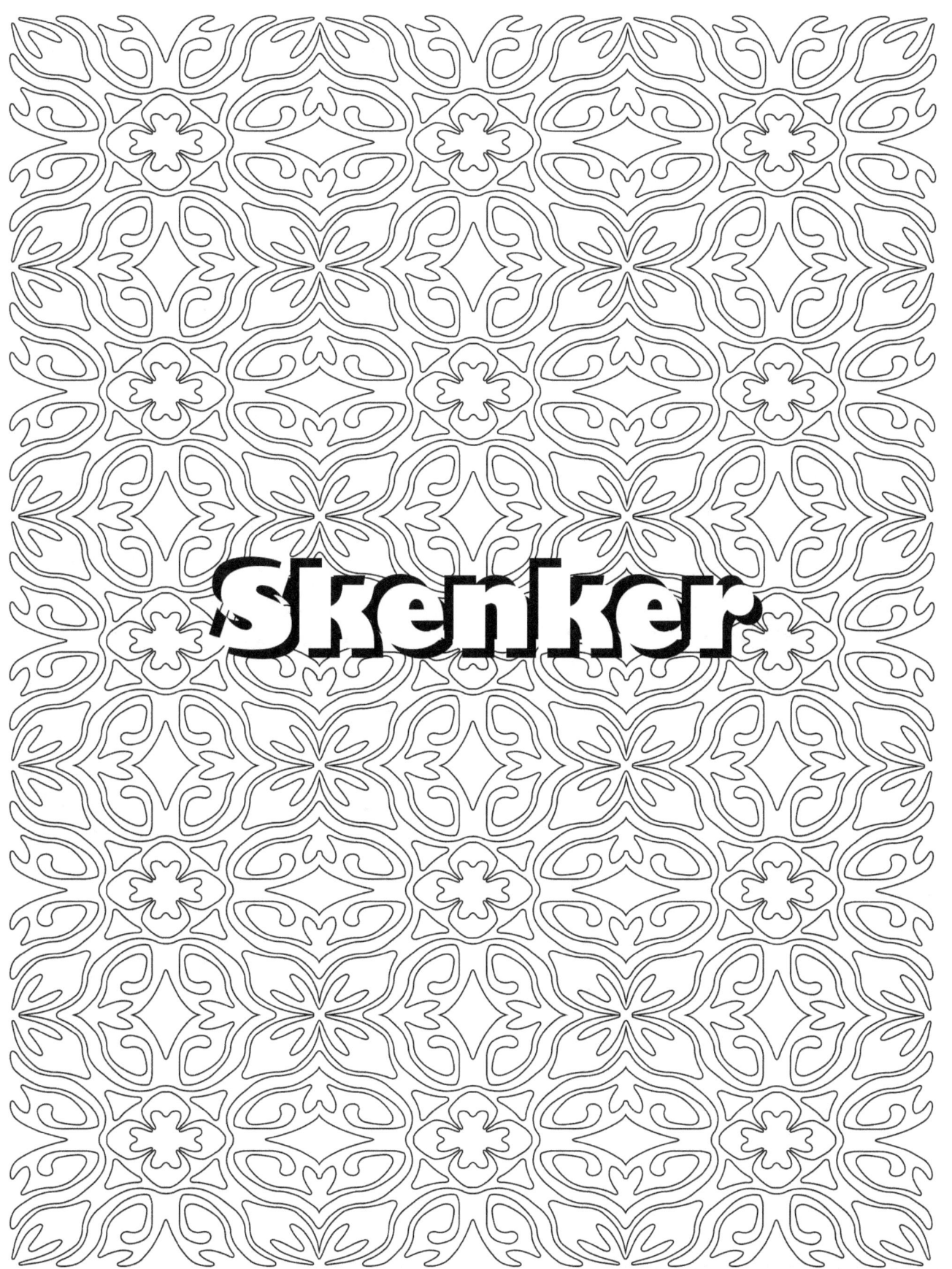

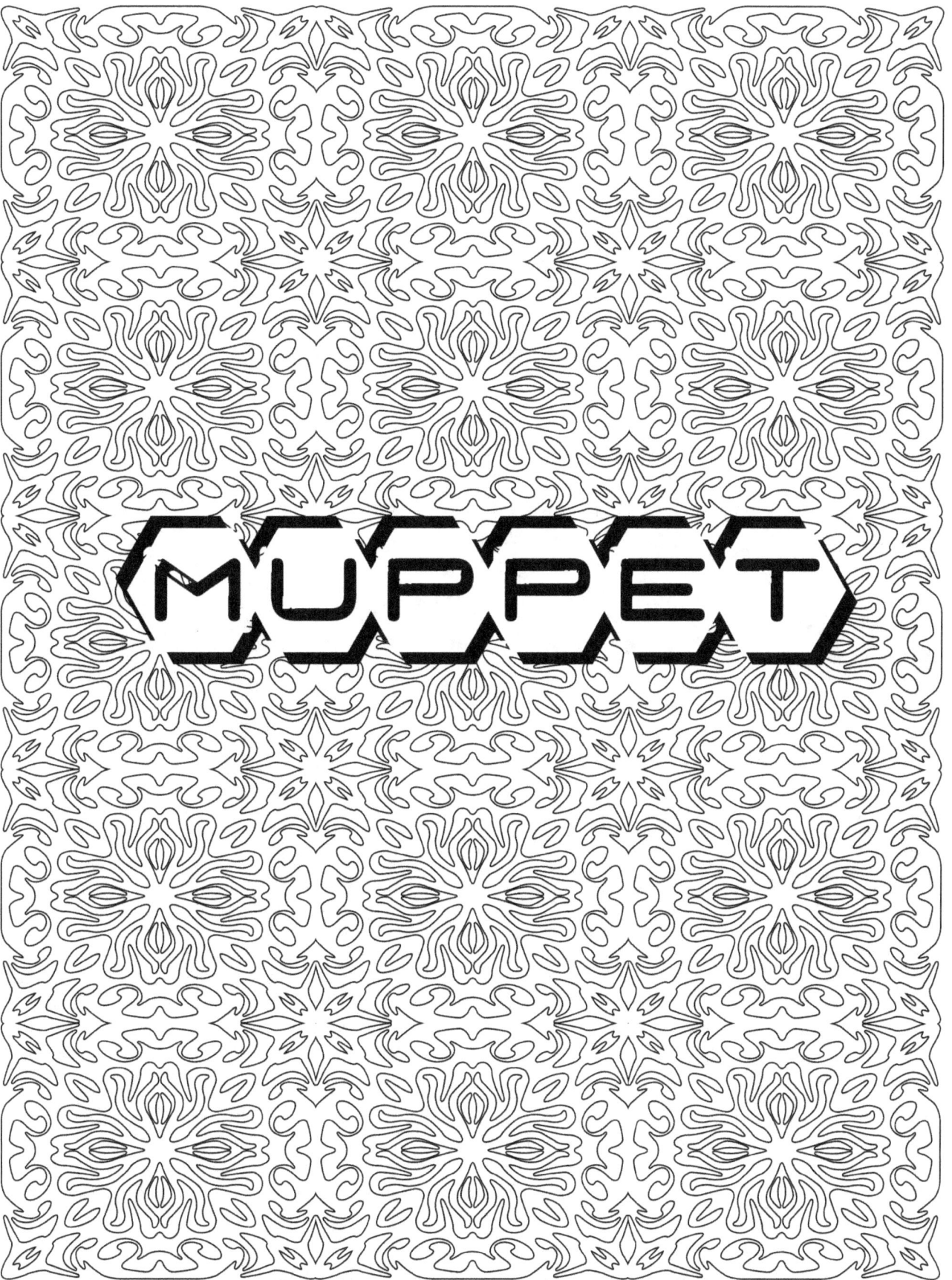

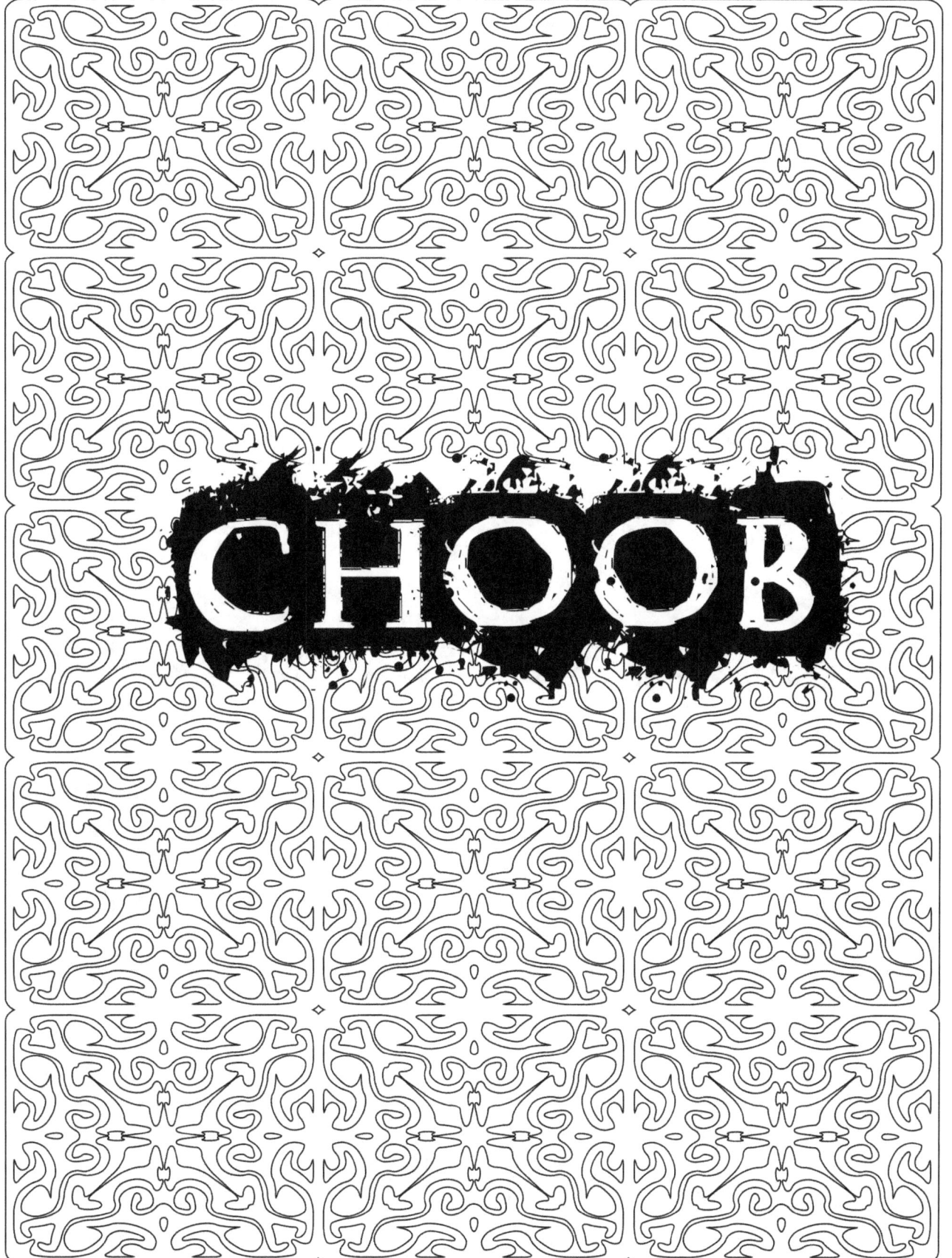

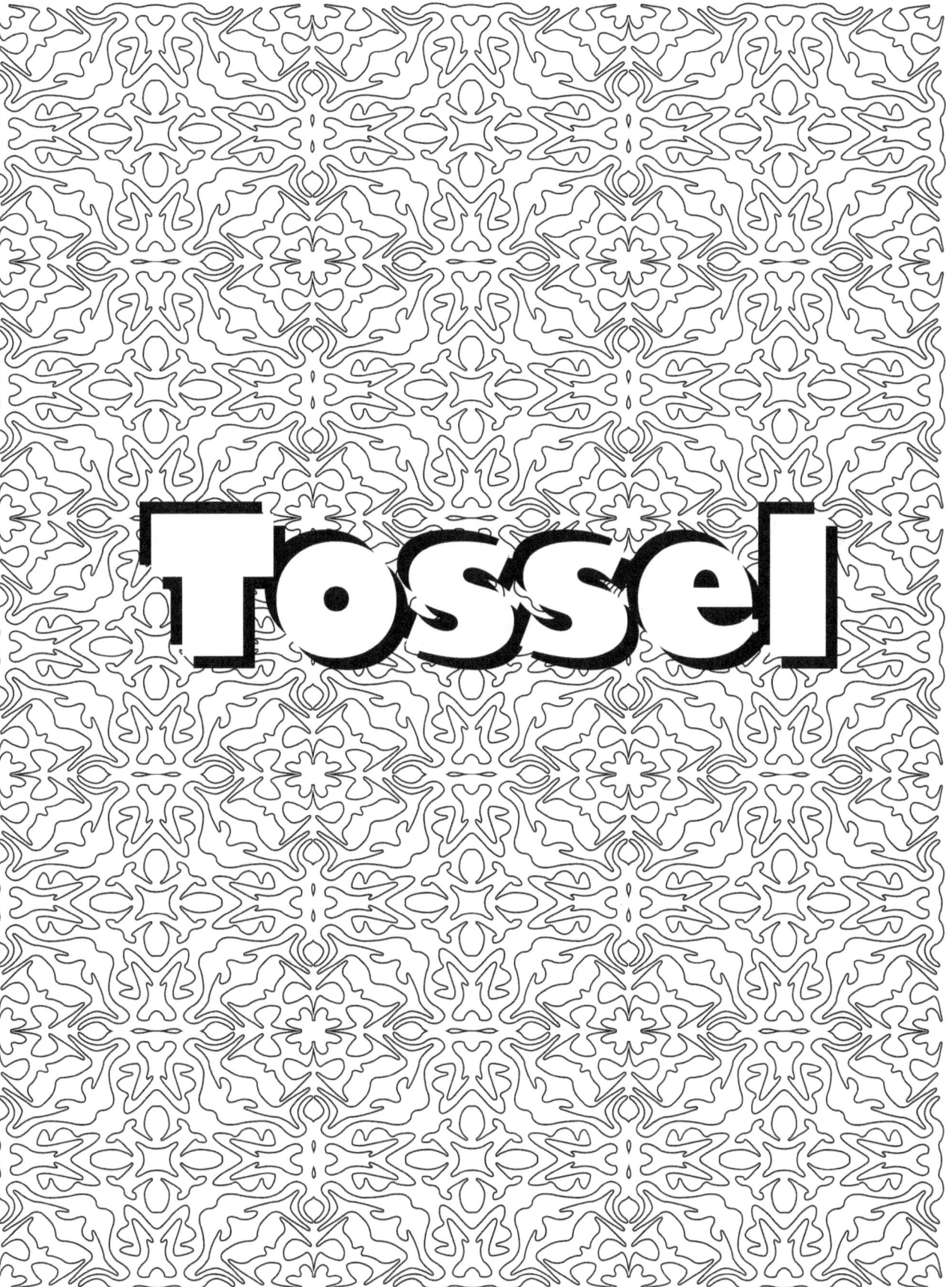

Final Words

Now Go Out There And Start Using Those Words!

Have Fun!

www.ingramcontent.com/pod-product-compliance
Lightning Source LLC
Chambersburg PA
CBHW081749220526
45468CB00008B/2304